Mark Irvine and Marion Cadman

Commercially Speaking

Workbook

OXFORD
UNIVERSITY PRESS

Oxford University Press
Great Clarendon Street, Oxford OX2 6DP

Oxford   New York
Auckland   Bangkok   Buenos Aires   Cape Town   Chennai
Dar es Salaam   Delhi   Hong Kong   Istanbul   Karachi
Kolkata   Kuala Lumpur   Madrid   Melbourne   Mexico City
Mumbai   Nairobi   São Paulo   Shanghai   Taipei   Tokyo
Toronto

OXFORD and OXFORD ENGLISH
are trade marks of Oxford University Press

ISBN 0 19 457232 3
© Oxford University Press 1999
Fifth impression 2004

No unauthorized photocopying

Printed in China

Acknowledgements
The authors and publisher are grateful to those who have given
permission to reproduce the following extracts and adaptations
of copyright material:

p 5 The Body Shop International plc for use of extracts from
Body and Soul by Anita Roddick, published by Vermilion 1991.
p 34 Incentives Two for use of extracts from 1998–99 catalogue.
pp 36 and 58 Sheil Land Associates Ltd. for use of extracts from
the *Penguin Dictionary of Jokes, Wisecracks, Quips and Quotes* by
Fred Metcalf. This compilation copyright © Fred Metcalf 1993.
p 38 SWIFT for use of extract from the SWIFT Annual Report
1996. p 43 Chartland Associates for use of Maximizer
Advertisement. p 44 *Business Life Magazine* for use of 'Files,
faxes and rock 'n' roll' by David Hewson, June 1997.
p 45 Ericsson and The Pocket Phone Shop for use of brochure
entries and pictures of Ericsson mobile phones. p 48 *Business
Life Magazine* for use of 'Take my card' by Helen Pickles, May
1997. p 52 The Excess Baggage Company for use of text and
diagrams from pamphlet, 1997. p 62 British Telecom for
information about and pictures of answering machines.
p 70 South London Press & Mercury Group for use of 'Going
for records' by Jeffrey Riley. Appeared in *Early Times*, March
1989. p 79 Natalie Graham / Times Newspapers Limited for use
of 'Towering success of dogged toy maker' by Natalie Graham.
Appeared in *The Sunday Times* 6 July 1997 © Times Newspapers
Limited, 1997.

The publishers would like to thank the following for permission
to reproduce photographs:

Brandmark Advertising p 43; British Telecommunications plc p
62 (Response 5 and Response 55); The Body Shop International
p 5 (Gilda Perella); Corbis UK Ltd pp 7 (Young 1920's adults),
10 (L'Aquila / John Heseltine); David Hartley Photography p 79
(Leslie Scott); Ericsson Limited p 45 (Mobile phone); Greg
Evans International pp 8 (Teenage group discussion), 21
(Receptionist on telephone), 65 (Female interviewing male);
Virgin Group p 70 (Virgin Megastore); Pictor International p 24
(Barbados); Robert Harding p 74 (Trade Fair); Russel Kientsch
p 44 (Jaye Müller); Tony Stone Images p 24 (Copenhagen / Tony
Craddock).

We would like to thank the following for their help and
co-operation:

Eastnor Pottery, First Direct, Barclays Bank.

Illustrations by:

Ned Jolliffe pp 11, 53
Harry Venning pp 4, 7, 36, 56, 58, 59, 61, 67, 76
Technical Graphics, OUP pp 17, 37, 49, 52

Studio Photography by Trevor Clifford p 22

Design by Sarah Tyzack

Contents

Introduction   4

Unit   1   5

Unit   2   10

Unit   3   16

Unit   4   22

Unit   5   28

Unit   6   34

Unit   7   40

Unit   8   46

Unit   9   52

Unit   10   58

Unit   11   64

Unit   12   70

Unit   13   76

Introduction

Could you run a business?
Do the questionnaire below and find out!

1 Do you enjoy:
- ☐ **a** thinking of new ideas?
- ☐ **b** following other people's instructions?
- ☐ **c** doing as little as possible?

2 In a difficult situation:
- ☐ **a** do you go out of the room?
- ☐ **b** do people expect that **you** will know what to do?
- ☐ **c** do you wait for someone to think of a solution?

3 Do you get colds or flu:
- ☐ **a** very often?
- ☐ **b** about three times a year?
- ☐ **c** very rarely?

4 When you have a problem, do you:
- ☐ **a** worry about it a lot?
- ☐ **b** try to forget about it?
- ☐ **c** try to solve it?

5 Think of the last time you did something wrong. Did you:
- ☐ **a** accept that you can't be perfect, but try to put it right?
- ☐ **b** say that it was someone else's fault?
- ☐ **c** feel miserable about it for weeks?

6 In a crisis do you:
- ☐ **a** see it as a challenge?
- ☐ **b** start to cry?
- ☐ **c** panic?

7 Do people say that you are:
- ☐ **a** kind but pessimistic?
- ☐ **b** aggressive?
- ☐ **c** confident and friendly?

8 Are you good at managing money? Do you:
- ☐ **a** have no idea how much money you have at any particular time?
- ☐ **b** know exactly how much money you have?
- ☐ **c** owe a lot of money to friends or family?

Unit 1

Section A

My mother's name is Gilda Perella. She was born in a small village near Cassino in *central* Italy, and came to England as a *nanny* when she was fifteen. She still *lives* in the house where I was born in 1942. It is called 'Atina', after her village, and has bright *red* window frames. Inside, it is very colourful too: the front *room* is full of little coloured *glass* ornaments. In the garden there are hundreds of flowers in *plastic* pots. It's incredible. I *think* she is incredible too.

1 Grammar

Read about the mother of famous businesswoman Anita Roddick. Tick (✓) the correct column in the table for each word in *italics* above.

	nouns	verbs	adjectives
central			✓
nanny			
lives			
red			
room			
glass			
plastic			
think			

2 Grammar

Is the word in italics a noun or a verb? Mark the sentences *N* (Noun) or *V* (Verb).

a 1 It was an interesting *talk*. ____

2 Can I *talk* to you? ____

b 1 I'd like to *travel* around Japan. ____

2 I love air *travel*. ____

c 1 The *use* of computers is essential. ____

2 Teresa loves to *use* her imagination. ____

d 1 I think I'm in *love*. ____

2 I *love* work. ____

e 1 I *work* eight hours a day. ____

2 I go to *work* by bus. ____

f 1 What *make* is your new car? ____

2 I want to *make* lots of money. ____

3 Grammar

What is the past simple of these verbs?

a belong _____

b stop _____

c die _____

d have _____

e love _____

f leave _____

g want _____

h make _____

i sell _____

4 Grammar

Complete each sentence with the correct form of a verb from this list:

have	travel	use	wear	sit	take

EXAMPLE

For me business is *wearing* special clothes.

a I think business is ⸺ behind a desk all day.

b I think business is ⸺ a secretary.

c For Peter business is ⸺ a lot.

d For Teresa business is ⸺ your imagination.

e For Silvia business is ⸺ risks.

Section B

1 Correspondence

Label the letter with these words:

salutation

signature

complimentary close

body of the letter

date

letterhead

a

Johnson & Jakes
CHARTERED ACCOUNTANTS

b 5 November 2000

c Dear Mr Bryars,

d I am writing to inform you that your account will in future be handled by Mr Crow, FCA. Ms French, who was in charge of your account, left our firm today and is now working in Paris. I trust this change is acceptable to you and hope we will continue to enjoy your custom for many years to come.

e Best regards,

f Peter Jakes

Peter Jakes

a ⸺

b ⸺

c ⸺

d ⸺

e ⸺

f ⸺

2 Grammar

What would you do in the following situations?

a You win a lottery. *I would* _____

_____

b You fail your final exams. _____

_____

c You pass your final exams. _____

_____

d You find some money in your classroom.

_____

_____

3 Grammar

Complete the text with prepositions.

When Giuseppe went ^{1}_____ London ^{2}_____ 1922 he had hope ^{3}_____ his heart but no money ^{4}_____ his pocket. He stayed ^{5}_____ relatives ^{6}_____ London for the first few years and worked ^{7}_____ a big clothes factory. Some of his friends came ^{8}_____ London and worked ^{9}_____ the same factory. ^{10}_____ Sundays they all went ^{11}_____ the country ^{12}_____ bicycles and had picnics. Giuseppe sent some money ^{13}_____ his family in Italy but he also put some money ^{14}_____ the bank and saved.

4 Grammar

Read the following letter from Peter to a friend telling him what has happened. Then write in the correct form of the verbs in brackets.

Dear Tom,

Amazing news! I'm rich! My mother's uncle

1 _____ (die) last month

and 2 _____ (leave) me

some money and a shop in London in his will.

The only problem is he

3 _____ (give) half of the

shop to another relative – a cousin in Italy.

Her name is Teresa.

I 4 _____ (not know) what

she 5 _____ (want) to do.

I don't know if she 6 _____

(speak) English. I 7 _____

(want) to go to London and open up the shop.

I think I 8 _____ (can)

make a lot of money in commerce – I like

meeting people and 9 _____

(buy) and 10 _____ (sell). My

mother says that 11 _____

(run) a shop is very hard work and the hours

are long and that there are a lot of risks.

I 12 _____ (like) hard work –

especially if I can 13 _____ (be) my

own boss. What do you think? What would you

do? 14 _____ (Write) soon

and tell me.

See you!

Peter

Section C

1 Reading

You and a group of friends are discussing what to do to earn some money for your holidays. Match these sentences with the correct gap in the dialogue:

a How about advertising?

b Why don't we try to find jobs?

c All right then – we could start an agency. We could offer different services.

d That's a good idea – and we can print some leaflets.

e And I could do decorating with my brother we're really good at that.

FRIEND Come on everyone – let's talk about this together. The problem is we all want to go on holiday but we need money. Any ideas?

YOU 1 _____

FRIEND But you know that's impossible – there are no jobs around.

YOU 2 _____

FRIEND That's not a bad idea – I could offer typing; I'm good at that.

YOU 3 _____

FRIEND Great – that's two different services already, and there are lots of other people who could help – Tim can cook, Annette can babysit, and Jack is marvellous with old people.

YOU 4 _____

FRIEND We could put an ad in the paper.

YOU 5 _____

FRIEND Yes, and we could use my father's computer to design them.

2 Telephoning

Tick (✔) the better response, 1 or 2, in each of the following situations.

a Could I speak to Mr Nichols, please?
- ☐ 1 That's I.
- ☐ 2 Speaking.

b Who's calling, please?
- ☐ 1 This is Jeff Peters, from Canada.
- ☐ 2 I'm Jeff, from Canada.

c Sorry, wrong number.
- ☐ 1 I'm afraid to disturb you.
- ☐ 2 Sorry to disturb you.

d I'd like to speak to the director.
- ☐ 1 I'm afraid he's meeting at the moment.
- ☐ 2 I'm afraid he's in a meeting at the moment.

3 Pronunciation

Look at the stress pattern in these words:

● •   • ●
orders   enjoy

Underline the word in each line that has a different stress pattern from the others.

a disturb	address	number	belong
b office	payment	speaking	idea
c mistake	wanted	message	legal
d discuss	London	surprise	consists
e inform	money	person	meeting

4 Language check

Translate the sentences into your language.

a For me business is about taking risks.

_____

b Do you think that money is important?

_____

c That's a good idea!

_____

d What about capital?

_____

e I regret to inform you …

_____

f Contact me as soon as possible.

_____

g Running a shop is very hard work.

_____

h I can understand your feelings.

_____

i I want to make a go of it.

_____

j Get real!

_____

Cover up each expression above and translate your sentence back into English.

Unit 2

Section A

1 Vocabulary

Below is some information about L'Aquila. Separate it into these categories. Write the correct number for each category.

1	climate
2	geography
3	transport and communications
4	history
5	industries
6	tourist attractions

a L'Aquila (population 65,000) is situated in the centre of Italy. __2__

b There is a motorway to Rome (99 kilometres long). __3__

c There is a company that makes equipment for telecommunications. __5__

d There is a colourful market, where tourists can buy souvenirs. ____

e It is 721 metres above sea level. ____

f There are some skiing resorts near the town. ____

g It lies in a valley surrounded by high mountains. ____

h It is near the Gran Sasso mountain. ____

i There are some pharmaceutical companies just outside the town. ____

j There are some excellent restaurants. ____

k It is 99 kilometres from the capital of Italy. ____

l The communications are good by road, but not by rail. ____

m There is no international airport. ____

n The town was founded in 1254. ____

o The weather is usually cold but dry in winter; and quite hot in summer. ____

p There is no major river near the town. ____

q The town was under Spanish rule for a long time. ____

2 Vocabulary

Write these numbers and percentages in words.

a 23

_____

_____

b 111

_____

_____

c 2,313

_____

_____

d 78,905

_____

_____

e 80.05%

_____

_____

f 100%

_____

g 205

_____

h 34.5

_____

i 12,560,000

_____

_____

3 Grammar

Tick (✔) the noun + noun expressions.

☐ **a** food bars

☐ **b** jazz music

☐ **c** excellent clubs

☐ **d** tram lines

☐ **e** old buildings

☐ **f** shopping centres

☐ **g** opera houses

☐ **h** sports centres

What else is there where you live? Write three more noun + noun expressions of your own.

_____

_____

_____

Section B

1 Correspondence

Mark the sentences *F* (Formal) or *I* (Informal).

a Thanks for your letter. It was great to hear from you. ——

b I am writing to ask for a catalogue of your new products. ——

c Can you tell me how to get to the hotel? ——

d Love to your family. ——

e I enclose a copy of the contract. ——

f See you next week. ——

2 Correspondence

Before Peter left Australia, Teresa wrote him the letter opposite. Complete it with these expressions.

a Can you send me …? ——

b You asked about … ——

c You also asked about … ——

d Looking forward to … ——

e Can you also let me know …? ——

f I enclose a … ——

3 Grammar

Cross out the word *to* where it is incorrect.

EXAMPLE
Can you ~~to~~ show me the way to the station?

a I would like to come to see you.

b I want to see the shop.

c Can I to help you?

d I can to help you tomorrow.

e Let me to know as soon as possible.

f Looking forward to meeting you.

Dear Peter,

It was lovely to speak to you on the phone. I hope you like L'Aquila. It is very different from Melbourne, I'm sure.

¹—— somewhere to stay. My father has an empty flat. You can use that. He doesn't want any rent for it.

²—— getting to L'Aquila. Don't worry! We can meet you at the airport. ³—— a photograph so we can recognize you? ⁴—— recent photo of me and my parents. ⁵—— your flight number and the exact time of your arrival.

⁶—— meeting you.

Teresa

4 Grammar

Look at the changes to this sentence:

I'm coming to London next week.
(not)   *I'm **not** coming to London next week.*
(you?)   ***Are you** coming to London next week?*
(Peter)   ***Peter is** coming to London next week.*
(Teresa / not) ***Teresa isn't** coming to London next week.*
(Peter?)   ***Is Peter** coming to London next week?*

Now change the following sentences in the same way:

a I'm interested in buying office furniture.

1 (not) _____ interested in buying office furniture.

2 (you?) _____ interested in buying office furniture?

3 (Peter) _____ interested in buying office furniture.

4 (Silvia / not) _____ interested in buying office furniture.

5 (he?) _____ interested in buying office furniture?

b I can come on Friday.

1 (not) _____ come on Friday.

2 (you?) _____ come on Friday?

3 (Silvia) _____ come on Friday.

4 (Marek / not) _____ come on Friday.

5 (they?) _____ come on Friday?

c I'd like to find a new job.

1 (not) _____ _____ find a new job.

2 (you?) _____ _____ find a new job?

3 (Peter) _____ _____ find a new job.

4 (Silvia / not) _____ _____ find a new job.

5 (Marek?) _____ _____ find a new job?

5 Reading

Complete the following fax with these words:

come	have	let	spend
have	know	lives	take

To: …

I'm hoping to [1] _____ to Warsaw to see you and talk about our project, so I would like to [2] _____ when the most suitable time is for you. I'm working on another project with a friend who also [3] _____ in Warsaw, so my plan is to visit both of you: you first and then my friend.

Can you please [4] _____ me know if the week beginning the 8th is convenient for you, and if you [5] _____ a preference for the beginning or the end of the week? Ideally, I'd like to [6] _____ a full day with you.

Can you also let me know how to get to your office from the airport? Is it far? How long does it [7] _____ by public transport? And do you [8] _____ any ideas about hotels in the centre of the city?

Yours sincerely,

Section C

1 Grammar

Do these verbs refer to the future or the present? Mark them *F* (Future) or *P* (Present).

a I'm coming on Monday. ——

b I'm phoning about a problem. ——

c He's seeing me tomorrow. ——

d We're leaving after the meeting. ——

e What are you doing now? ——

f I'm finishing this letter. ——

g What are you doing before the meeting? ——

h I'm talking to some visitors after lunch. ——

2 Grammar

Rewrite these sentences with contracted forms.

EXAMPLE
I would like to see you.
I'd like to see you.

a I have started.

_____

b It has been changed.

_____

c He is arriving late.

_____

d She is coming after the meeting.

_____

e He would like to come.

_____

3 Grammar

Write in contracted forms where possible. The first one has been done for you. There are nine more examples.

name's
'My name is Anastasia. I am Polish but I live in the USA. I have got three brothers and one sister. I have never been to Poland but I would like to go there some day and visit my relatives. My aunt and uncle live in Warsaw. They are coming to visit us this summer and we are looking forward to seeing them very much. My mother has decorated a room specially for them, and she is cooking lots of Polish specialities and putting them in the freezer so they will be ready.'

4 Telephoning

Complete these sentences with *afraid* or *sorry*.

a I'm _____, I'm _____ I can't speak Spanish very well.

b I'm _____, can you say that again, please?

c I'm _____, did you say John or Jack?

d 'Can you both come?' 'I'm _____ not.'

5 Telephoning

Put the words in the correct order. Use contractions where you can.

EXAMPLE
coming flight am I on different a
I'm coming on a different flight.

a coming you are when

_____

b leaving I Rome am the tenth March of on

_____

_____

c more speak you please slowly can

_____

d together are coming you

_____

e can too Peter come

_____

f he the arriving next is day

_____

g say you please can again that

_____

6 Language check

Translate the sentences into your language.

a I can't wait to go to London.

_____

b I remember lots of music shops with millions of CDs.

_____

_____

c I am writing with reference to your advertisement.

_____

_____

d I look forward to hearing from you.

_____

e Let me know the exact time of your arrival.

_____

f I am coming on a different day.

_____

g When are you coming?

_____

h We are leaving Rome on the first of May.

_____

_____

i Sorry, could you repeat that, please?

_____

j It is very kind of you.

_____

Cover up each expression above and translate your sentence back into English.

Unit 3

Section A

1 Reading

Complete the text with these verbs.

are	buy	go	live	sell
be	do	have	open	want

What is a good location for a shop?

When you want to open a shop, you must study its location carefully. For example, what do the other shops in the immediate area ¹_____ ? Sometimes it can help *your* business if there are other similar shops near you because many customers prefer to ²_____ to a location with two or more shops that sell similar products.

The population near the shop can also ³_____ of vital importance: you mustn't think that it is always easy to persuade people to come far to your particular shop. And what sort of people ⁴_____ near the shop? Do they ⁵_____ a lot of money? If you want to sell your products in large quantities, you need to be in a large population centre.

If you only ⁶_____ to sell to particular sections of the market, you may need to find an area with a specific type of population. For example, if you intend to ⁷_____ a bookshop, you will want to be in a town of a certain size. You also need a population with a lot of people who ⁸_____ books, for example, students.

Another important consideration is how many potential customers pass the shop every day – on their way to work, or when they ⁹_____ their other shopping. It can be a good idea to test this yourself by standing outside the shop on days which are usually busy and on days which ¹⁰_____ usually quiet.

2 Grammar

Read about Middlemarch and complete the questions below.

Then answer your questions, using the information from the advert.

Come to
MIDDLEMARCH
THE IDEAL PLACE FOR YOUR BUSINESS
Middlemarch is in the
HEART OF ENGLAND.

❖ It has a number of factories and a very good shopping mall.
❖ There are also excellent sports facilities because the town has a new football stadium and an Olympic swimming pool.
❖ It has also got some of the best parkland in the country.
❖ It is in the centre of a vast communications network and has easy access to four important motorways.

Life is better in Middlemarch,
business is easier,
and your employees are happier.

a Where _____ Middlemarch?

_____

b Does it _____ good shopping facilities?

_____

c What sports facilities has it _____ ?

_____

d ____ it near beautiful countryside?

_____

e _____ it have access to motorways?

_____

3 Grammar

Complete these sentences with *it* or *there*.

a —— are thousands of shops in London.

b —— is a very exciting city.

c —— is no toilet in Giuseppe's shop.

d —— is very dark.

e —— is going to be light and bright.

f —— is a lot of competition in London.

g —— is a very busy city.

4 Grammar

In the following sentences change the form of the verb *have*.

EXAMPLE
Has your mother got a car?
Does your mother have a car?

a I've got three sisters.

_____

b Has she got a flat in London?

_____

c They haven't any friends.

_____

d Does London have a drugs problem?

_____

e Have you got a moment?

_____

5 Vocabulary

Complete the table below.

Measurements	
a long	*length*
b wide	
c high	
d deep	

6 Vocabulary

Write these measurements in words.

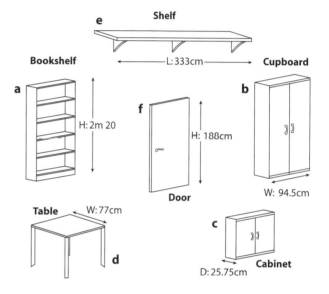

a *The bookshelf is two metres twenty high.*

b _____

_____

c _____

_____

d _____

_____

e _____

_____

f _____

_____

7 Grammar

Underline the nouns which are countable.

advice	commerce	information
list	money	pound
product	shelf	supplier
T-shirt	telephone	thing
window	wood	

8 Grammar

Complete these questions with *many* or *much*.

a How _____ wood do we need?

b How _____ shelves do we have?

c How _____ suppliers are we looking for?

d How _____ money can you give me?

e How _____ information did they give you?

f How _____ windows are there in the shop?

9 Vocabulary

The word chain below has words for things you can find in an office or shop *and* things you *don't* usually find there.

a Separate the words.
computerstationeryfaxmachinebedcatdoghifitele
visionfilingcabinetprintermonkeyfridgebookshel
vestelephonesofaparrotflowersplantsdocumentsh
redderashtraymousevideocalculatorumbrellastan
dcanarycalendarchequebookdiaryrubberpenspen
cilsfiles

b Cross out all the things you *don't* usually find in an office.

Section B

1 Correspondence

Choose the correct answer. The purpose of the letter below is _____.

a to ask for financial help.
b a letter to a friend.
c to ask for a catalogue.

Cross out everything that is irrelevant.

> Dear Sir,
>
> I am living in England with my cousin. He's from Canada and his name is Jimmy Peterson. He's very good with his hands and he repairs clocks and watches. I would like to open a clock shop with him. He could repair clocks and watches in the back room and I could sell new ones. And I could organize the repairs: take people's names and addresses, etc., etc. We want to buy some watches from you, so we need a catalogue and a price list. We want to sell to older people but we think the market for watches for children and teenagers is bigger so can you send us lots of information and *pictures of watches made of plastic in bright colours with pictures on them*. Thank you.
>
> Yours faithfully,
>
> Giorgio Marchetti
>
> PS We are planning to open the shop very soon so can you send the catalogue as soon as possible?

2 Correspondence

Rewrite the letter clearly and simply, using the outline below to help you.

> Dear Sir,
>
> My cousin and I are planning to
> _____
> _____
> _____ soon.
> Could you please send us your
> new _____
> _____ ?
> We are particularly interested
> in watches for _____
> _____
> and would like some
> information about watches
> made of _____
> _____
>
> Yours faithfully,
>
> Giorgio Marchetti

3 Vocabulary

Separate the following descriptive adjectives:

Polisholdroundwoollensilksmallnewgreenglassbig
TurkishlittleplasticmetalsquareenormousSpanish
HungarianFrenchGermanleathergreyovalwhite
oblong

Sort the words into these categories:

size	shape	age

colour	nationality	material

4 Correspondence

Tick (✓) the formal expressions.

- ☐ **a** Hi!
- ☐ **b** Here I am again!
- ☐ **c** I am writing in reply to your letter of October 1st.
- ☐ **d** Thanks for your letter. It was great to hear from you.
- ☐ **e** Could you please let me know which date would be most convenient for our next meeting?
- ☐ **f** Hope you are all well.

Section C

1 Telephoning

Reply to the telephone requests below.

EXAMPLE
Can you please tell him I called?
Yes, I'll tell him.

a Could you send me a copy of your brochure,

please? _____ one immediately.

b Can you please fax me a price for three display

units? _____ this
afternoon.

c Could you call back this afternoon, please?

Yes, _____ at three o'clock.

2 Telephoning

Complete the table opposite with these phrases:

Hold the line, please.
Mark Peters here.
I'd like to speak to ...
This is Ann Jones.
I'm afraid she isn't in the office at the moment.
Can you put me through to ....?
Will you hold?
Mrs Jones is in a meeting at the moment.
I'm afraid her line's engaged.
Just a moment.
Could I speak to ..., please?
Ann Jones speaking.
Can I speak to ..., please?
I'm afraid he's not available.
One moment, please.

Getting through on the telephone

Saying who you are

Mark Peters here.

_____

_____

_____

Asking to speak to someone

_____

_____

_____

_____

Asking a caller to wait

Hold the line, please.

_____

_____

_____

_____

Explaining someone isn't available

_____

_____

_____

_____

3 Telephoning

Rewrite **A**'s lines with the words in the correct order.

A morning good. I speak to Mr could please Smithson?

_____

_____

B Sorry, I didn't catch that. Who did you want to speak to?
A Jack Smithson. is my name Anna Larosa.

_____

_____

B I'm putting you through.
A repeat that please sorry could you. I'm afraid don't understand I English on the telephone very well.

_____

_____

_____

B (_repeats slowly_) I'm putting you through to Mr Smithson.
A you thank.

_____

4 Language check

Translate the sentences into your language.

a Is there enough light for a shop?

_____

b How long is this wall?

_____

c What size do you need?

_____

d Please could you send us replacements as soon as possible.

_____

_____

e Who's calling, please?

_____

f I'll call back at about four o'clock.

_____

g I'm afraid the line's engaged.

_____

h I'll tell him you called.

_____

i Will you hold?

_____

j I'm putting you through.

_____

Cover up each expression above and translate your sentence back into English.

Unit 4

Section A

1 Vocabulary

Complete the text opposite with these adjectives:

cheap	expensive	important	top
excellent	fashionable	real	

TERESA I like ¹_____ quality things and I like to look ²_____ . I prefer to have few things but all the best makes. The make is very ³_____ to me. I really don't like ⁴_____ imitations. For me, it is better to wait if you don't have enough money; and then, when you do have enough money, to buy the ⁵_____ thing. I love to give presents too. And I think the person you give a present to should know it was ⁶_____, that it cost you a lot of money. A designer label is an ⁷_____ way of being sure about this.

2 Vocabulary

Complete the text below with these adjectives:

best	important	interested	ridiculous
designer	individual	recycled	

PETER I'm not ¹_____ in designer clothes, and designer labels are not ²_____ to me. For example, I think it is absolutely ³_____ to buy pens and exercise books with designer labels. Surely it must be better to buy ⁴_____ paper and to think about the environment? When I give a present, I like to think hard about the person I'm giving it to and to choose something really ⁵_____ . The cost is not really important, but I prefer to look for things in markets. In fact, I often find the ⁶_____ presents in second-hand markets. I really don't like the way Teresa tries to impress people with ⁷_____ labels. For me, that's not being individual. It's like being in a uniform.

3 Grammar

You want to know how people feel about stationery – and in particular, about designer pens and exercise books. Use the following suggestions to write questions in the present simple for a market research questionnaire on people's tastes and habits.

a How much / spend on exercise books?
b How many exercise books / buy in a year?
c the cover – important to you?
d cartoons on the cover / like?
e photographs on the cover / like?
f How / choose a pen: by the quality of the ink or by its appearance?
g What / the most you pay for a pen?
h What / the most you pay for an exercise book?
i people / give them to you as presents?

4 Vocabulary

Write these prices as words.

EXAMPLE
15p *fifteen pence*

a £30

_____.

b £150

_____

c F3.50

_____

d Lire 2,000,000

_____

e $20.50

_____

f 2,500 pesetas

_____

_____

g 6,000 DM

_____

a _____
b _____
c _____
d _____
e _____
f _____
g _____
h _____
i _____

5 Grammar

Complete the sentences below with these words:

the	in	than	than	in

a Peter is older _____ Teresa.

b Teresa speaks better English _____ most of her Italian friends.

c At school she was the best at English _____ the class.

d Yesterday she bought the most expensive dress _____ the shop.

e And Peter bought _____ least expensive pair of jeans.

6 Grammar

Write sentences comparing the following:

a These birthday presents: a book / a weekend at Disneyland Paris
(Use the adjectives *cheap* and *exciting*)

A book is cheaper than a weekend at

Disneyland Paris. A weekend ...

_____

b These cities: Prague / Washington
(Use the adjectives *small* and *modern*)

_____

_____

_____

c These places: Copenhagen / Barbados
(Use the adjectives *cool* and *exotic*)

_____

_____

_____

7 Vocabulary

Solve the clues and find the missing word.

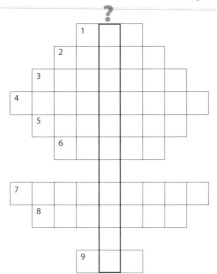

1 Verb – to be the best or first in a competition.
2 Adjective – better than 'fine'.
3 A written confirmation of an agreement is in

w_____.

4 Think of Australia and you might think of this.
5 Peter _____ work when he was eighteen.
6 The shop _____ new furniture. We can get some today.
7 Sentences which ask for information.
8 Drawings / ideas for making things.
9 Noun – this tells us how old something or someone is.

Can you find the missing word?

Write a clue for it.

_____

_____

Section B

1 Grammar

Put the verbs in the advert in the present simple or the present continuous.

> ### Cotton on – the natural way!
>
> Our company [1]_____ (specialize) in manufacturing bright and attractive shirts in natural fibres. We only [2]_____ (use) top quality materials. At the moment we [3]_____ (work) on a new range for the autumn. We [4]_____ (make) radical changes in the design team and [5]_____ (hope) you will like our new-look products. We [6]_____ (believe) in quality and always [7]_____ (do) our best to produce new and vibrant designs . This year we [8]_____ (produce) over fifty new designs in great colours. Our customers [9]_____ (know) they can rely on us!

2 Correspondence

The second paragraph of a letter of enquiry usually contains a specific enquiry or request, for example, about catalogues, prices, or technical information.

Underline the information or material requested in these extracts.

EXAMPLE
Will you please let us have some technical information about your new models?

a We would very much appreciate a copy of your latest price list.
b Would you kindly send us some samples for inspection by return post?
c Please let me know as soon as possible if you can offer us a 10% discount.
d We would be pleased to know your delivery terms and method of payment.

3 Reading

Look at the advertisement for Visionwide below and find the expressions in *italics* which explain that:

a you can have what you want very quickly.

_____

b they will store your negatives for you.

_____

c they will take photographs for you.

_____

d they can do a lot of different things.

_____

e they will improve the quality of your original.

_____

> ### Photographic printing
>
> All the advantages of a fully equipped West End photographic lab. With 25 years' experience of producing publicity and promotional prints, Visionwide are the professionals' choice with *a wide range of services* including:
>
> * Specialist printing
> * Black & white and colour printing, from negative, transparency & flat copy
> * Copy transparencies from flat artwork
> * *Digital retouching*
> * Digital scanning, manipulation & output
> * Duplicate transparencies
> * *Studio photography*
> * Film processing
> * *Free negative filing*
> * *Fast turnaround, from 4 to 48 hours*

4 Correspondence

Imagine that you are a young fashion photographer. Read the list of services offered by Visionwide, decide which services you are interested in, and write to enquire about prices and discounts.

USEFUL LANGUAGE
Dear Sir,
I saw your advertisement in …
Could you please send me … ?
Would you kindly send me … ?
Please can you let me have … ?
Yours faithfully,

Section C

1 Telephoning

Match each expression with a gap in the telephone conversation below.

a I'm sorry, I didn't catch that.
b what kind of shop is it?
c Hold on, please.
d Thanks for your help.
e But could you please send us a letter?
f I'm thinking of opening a shop in London.
g What kind of help would you like?

SWITCHBOARD	Spanish Embassy. Can I help you?
PETER	Could I speak to someone in the Commercial Office, please?
SWITCHBOARD	¹_____ I'm putting you through.
TRADE ATTACHÉ	Commercial Office. Can I help you?
PETER	Yes. My name is Peter Clapton. ²_____ and I would like some information from you, please.
TRADE ATTACHÉ	Right, a shop. Now, ³_____ .
PETER	The idea at the moment is to open a gift shop selling products from all around the world.
TRADE ATTACHÉ	What products do you have in mind?
PETER	Er, from Spain: castanets, ornaments, silk shawls ... and, er ... we're not really sure what else.
TRADE ATTACHÉ	⁴_____ .
PETER	Information about possible suppliers.
TRADE ATTACHÉ	⁵_____ .
PETER	Information about possible suppliers.
TRADE ATTACHÉ	Yes, we can help. ⁶_____ And could you specify exactly what products you have in mind?
PETER	Certainly, I'll put a letter in the post.
TRADE ATTACHÉ	And could you address the letter to me by name, that's Miguel Jiménez.
PETER	OK. ⁷_____ . Bye.
TRADE ATTACHÉ	Goodbye.

2 Telephoning

Which of the expressions below:

1 explain why the people are calling?
2 make a specific request / enquiry?

Mark each sentence *1* or *2*.

a I'm calling about an order. _____

b I'm interested in buying some of your new range. _____

c Can you give me a quote? _____

d I'm ringing about a problem with an invoice. _____

e What is your best price? _____

f Could you give me a quotation? _____

g I'm phoning about your advertisement in *The Times*. _____

h Can you give me your best price on that? _____

i I'm ringing for some information. _____

j How much is model XYZ? _____

k How much does model PQS cost? _____

l How much would it cost for a hundred? _____

3 Telephoning

Rewrite these numbers in figures.

EXAMPLE
five oh   *50*

a one five _____

b two oh double four _____

c six oh _____

d oh one eight one _____

e one three _____

4 Vocabulary

Look at the dictionary entry below.

> **love** [U] /lʌv/ *n* a very strong feeling of affection.
> *opp.* hate

Write questions about the word *love*. Then match the answers to your questions from the list below.

EXAMPLE
Ask about the grammatical form.
Is the word countable or uncountable?
It's uncountable.

a Ask about the pronunciation.

_____

_____

b Ask about the spelling.

_____

_____

c Ask about the meaning.

_____

d Ask about the opposite.

_____

– It means a very strong feeling of affection.
– Hate.
– It is uncountable.
– /lʌv/.
– L–O–V–E.

Write answers for questions **a–d** about the word *succeed*.

> **succeed** /sək'siːd/ *v* to do what you wanted or
> tried to do, *opp.* fail

a _____

b _____

c _____

d _____

5 Language check

Translate the sentences into your language.

a Can you give us a price for these T-shirts, please?

_____

_____

b Is fashion important to you?

_____

c The green ones are the cheapest.

_____

_____

d I was given your name by Mr Smith.

_____

e I am opening a shop soon.

_____

f I am interested in knowing more about your service.

_____

_____

g What does 'invoice' mean?

_____

h How do you pronounce this word?

_____

i We need fifteen boxes a.s.a.p.

_____

_____

j This is Mr Peters speaking.

_____

Cover up each expression above and translate your sentence back into English.

Unit 5

Section A

1 Reading

Read about these people. Who would you like to introduce to whom? Underline the information you think appropriate to mention when introducing them in a business context.

George Elder has long hair and blue eyes. When he was young he was a football player. He lives in Spain now with his wife and three children. He has a prosperous business importing British food to Spain for supermarkets. He is 42 years old and an Arsenal supporter. He is interested in expanding his business interests to building holiday homes on the Costa Brava.

Joan Hardy lives in London with her husband and two children. She has a very good job as head of marketing for a large clothes manufacturer. She has a very busy life and travels a lot. One of her problems is that she needs someone to live in and look after the children after school and in emergencies. She has a beautiful house in Highbury and a large garden. She likes going to the theatre.

Marie Stères lives in Marseilles. She studied English at school but doesn't speak it very well. She would like to spend a year in England and learn the language really well. She is 19 and has three brothers and she loves children. She likes making her own clothes and would like to be a tailor when she is older.

Antonio Heráldez is Spanish. He is from a noble old family. He is a popular singer and guitarist and often appears on television. His family used to own land on the Costa Brava but they have sold most of it now. Antonio needs some money quickly as his daughter is getting married next year and he will have to give a big party. He has some land left in a development area and he is interested in selling it or developing it.

2 Writing

Write two dialogues in which you introduce the people in **1** to each other. Start like this:

YOU   *A*, I'm sure you'd like to meet *B*. He / she ...
A   How interesting! Pleased to meet you, *B*.
YOU   And this is *A*. He / she ...

3 Vocabulary

Tick (✔) the questions which you consider appropriate during a first conversation with a business acquaintance.

- ☐ **a** Which political party do you support?
- ☐ **b** How much do you earn?
- ☐ **c** How did you start in this line of business?
- ☐ **d** Can we meet again?
- ☐ **e** Here is my card.
- ☐ **f** Do you have any trouble with tax authorities?
- ☐ **g** Would you like to visit my factory?
- ☐ **h** Are you well connected – from a good family?
- ☐ **i** Business is really bad – I really don't know what to do.
- ☐ **j** This is an exciting time in our business.

4 Grammar

Make questions to ask someone about what they have done in their life.

EXAMPLE
ever / work / office?
Have you ever worked in an office?

a ever / sell / things in a street market?

_____

_____

b ever / go / to India?

_____

c ever / make / a really important decision?

_____

_____

d ever / study / accounting?

_____

e ever / surf / the Internet for more than an hour?

_____

f ever / use / a photocopier?

_____

g ever / speak / to a sales rep?

_____

5 Vocabulary

Draw a line to link the beginnings and endings of the questions below. Use each ending once only.

a Have you ever been	**1** anything really unusual?
b Have you ever bought	**2** sure that you were doing the right thing?
c Have you ever done	**3** a present which was very expensive?
d Have you ever eaten	**4** to a politician?
e Have you ever felt	**5** a really famous person?
f Have you ever had to	**6** to an unusual shop?
g Have you ever met	**7** work on national holidays?
h Have you ever put	**8** money in a bank?
i Have you ever written	**9** in unpleasant company?

6 Grammar

Rewrite these questions, adding *yet* or *ever* in the correct place.

EXAMPLE
Have you written the letter to the bank?
Have you written the letter to the bank yet?

a Have you been to an opera house?

_____

b Has your partner decided what to do?

_____

c Have you met anyone famous?

_____

d Has your mother seen the new house?

_____

e Have you heard from the new supplier?

_____

7 Grammar

Look at the changes to this sentence:

I want to sell to large organizations.
(not) *I don't want* to sell to large organizations.
(you?) *Do you want* to sell to large organizations?
(Peter) *Peter wants* to sell to large organizations.
(Teresa / not) *Teresa doesn't want* to sell to large organizations.
(Silvia?) *Does Silvia want* to sell to large organizations?
Now change the following sentences in the same way:

a I need to buy more supplies.

1 (not) _____ buy more supplies.

2 (Peter?) _____ buy more supplies?

3 (Silvia / not) _____ buy more supplies.

4 (you?) _____ buy more supplies?

5 (they) _____ buy more supplies.

b I trust him.

1 (you?) _____ trust him?

2 (Peter / not) _____ trust him.

3 (Marek) _____ trust him.

4 (not) _____ trust him.

5 (Silvia?) _____ trust him?

c I'm prepared to work harder.

1 (Peter) _____ work harder.

2 (not) _____ work harder.

3 (you?) _____ work harder?

4 (Silvia / not) _____ work harder.

5 (we) _____ work harder.

d I've finished the letter.

1 (not) _____ finished the letter.

2 (you?) _____ finished the letter?

3 (Marek) _____ finished the letter.

4 (Silvia?) _____ finished the letter?

5 (Peter / not) _____ finished the letter.

8 Vocabulary

Solve these anagrams and then put the words in the sentences below.

RMEANTGEE	SOLS
ALCPTAI	KCLAB NAD HTWEI
PPIAHRSTREN	FTPRIO

If you invest [1]c_____l in a business but then the business goes bankrupt, you make a [2]l_____s .
If you invest in a business and the business goes well, you make a [3]p_____t.
Before you start a [4]p_____p with other investors, you should have a written [5]a_____t, which stipulates everything in [6]b_____e.

Section B

1 Correspondence

Read the two replies about possible gifts to sell in Teresa and Peter's shop and fill in the table.

	Wrap-it-up	Eastnor Pottery
a How many leaflets / brochures are enclosed?		
b Is there a price list?		
c Are there any samples enclosed?		
d Is an exclusive design / logo possible?		
e If so, how much does it cost?		
f Is a discount offered or mentioned?		
g Is a minimum order mentioned?		

Eastnor Pottery
CONTEMPORARY CERAMICS

Clock Cottage
Home Farm
Eastnor
Ledbury
Herefordshire
HR8 1RD

Telephone|Fax
01531 633255

Dear Teresa Volpe,

Thank you for your letter of 5 February, requesting details of our pottery.

I am enclosing a colour brochure and price list covering our standard range. I have also enclosed a colour leaflet about our Specials. For a design charge of £100 you may have your own exclusive design put on selected items of pottery.

Please also find enclosed our leaflet on the very popular 'Honey Bee' range of pottery. We introduced this range towards the end of last year and it has proved to be a very good seller.

If I can be of any further assistance to you, please do not hesitate to get in touch. For export we are willing to offer a discount of 30%.

Yours sincerely,

John Williams

John Williams

Wrap-it-up

59 Queen Street   Reading   Berkshire   RG7 2LP
Tel: (01734) 592522   Fax: (01734) 592521

Dear Teresa Volpe,

Thank you for your recent enquiry about 'Wrap-it-up' packaging. Please find enclosed a price list, brochure and some design samples.

We supply beautiful gift packaging in a wide range of designs and colours at a competitive price. Our handmade gift bags come in 12 sizes and over 30 designs, and all have our special 'Wrap-it-up' gift tag. We also make gift boxes for chocolates, and accessory products.

We can design packaging exclusively for your company, and can include your company logo. The logo can be printed on any of our packaging. We charge £40 for a logo plate.

Our minimum order is £50, and we offer discounts for larger orders.

Please do not hesitate to contact me if you require further information.

I look forward to hearing from you soon.

Yours sincerely,

Emma Marshall

Emma Marshall

2 Correspondence

Number the parts of this letter in the correct order.

a _____

Yours sincerely,

b _____

We base our discounts on the retail value of each order. A copy of the schedule is enclosed, and all transport and postage costs will be charged to your account.

c _____

Thank you for your letter of 6 February.

d _____

We trust the above information is of assistance.

e _____

We can either supply orders on credit terms of 90 days or pre-payment terms, i.e. on receipt of your payment for the value of the order, plus the cost of the postage. To open an account with credit terms, we require details of your banker and two trade references.

f _____

Please find enclosed a copy of our current catalogue and order form / price list for your perusal.

g _____

Dear Peter Clapton,

3 Grammar

Complete the letter below using some of the words from this list:

add	adding	receive	receiving
complete	completing	return	returning
enclose	enclosing	send	sending
hope	hoping	thank	thanking

Gift Finder

5 St Stephen's Lane
London SW6 9EF
Tel: (0171) 767 7566
Fax: (0171) 767 7567
e-mail: giftfind@sew.co.uk

Dear Sir / Madam

¹ _____ you for your kind enquiry.

I have pleasure in ² _____ a sample copy of *The Gift Finder*, which I ³ _____ you will find interesting.

I also enclose an order form for you to ⁴ _____ and ⁵ _____ if you wish to subscribe to the journal. Please ⁶ _____ it along with your remittance to the address on the form. I will then ⁷ _____ your name to our mailing list so that you will ⁸ _____ *The Gift Finder* regularly every month.

Yours faithfully

S. Jacobs

S. Jacobs
The Gift Finder
Subscription Department

Section C

1 Telephoning

Tick (✓) the most appropriate response in each case.

a Could I speak to Mr Smith, please?
- ☐ 1 No, you can't.
- ☐ 2 I'm afraid Mr Smith isn't available at the moment.
- ☐ 3 He isn't here.

b Can you tell me when he'll be in?
- ☐ 1 No, I can't tell you that.
- ☐ 2 He didn't say.
- ☐ 3 I'm afraid I really don't know. I'm sorry.

c Oh, I really need to speak to him.
- ☐ 1 Would you like me to take a message?
- ☐ 2 As I told you, he's not available today.
- ☐ 3 He's very busy.

d Please tell him I called and ask him to get back to me.
- ☐ 1 I'm telling him your message.
- ☐ 2 If I see him, I'll tell him.
- ☐ 3 I'll make sure he gets your message.

e Good. Thank you.
- ☐ 1 What's your name again? ... And you didn't give me your number.
- ☐ 2 You're welcome. Can I just check your name and number?
- ☐ 3 I need your name and number to give him your message. Give me them please.

2 Telephoning

Read the following conversation as Ms Peters takes a message for her colleague. Complete the message form.

A Hello. Could I speak to Mrs Johnson, please?
B I'm afraid she isn't in the office this morning. This is Anne Peters speaking. Can I give her a message?
A Yes. Tell her I called about the meeting tomorrow. I really need to speak to her before the meeting. Can you get her to call me?
B Certainly, but I'm afraid I don't know your name.
A Sorry. It's Jack Roberts, from Compute 4 You.
B Can I have your number, please?
A It's OK. She knows my number.
B Right – but could you give it to me – just to be sure.
A OK. It's 0171–876–9934.

Message for: _____

From: _____

Number: _____

Message: _____

_____

_____

Message taken by _____

at *10.30*   on *Thursday*

---

3 Language check

Translate the sentences into your language.

a I'd like you to meet Silvia.

_____

b Pleased to meet you.

_____

c Is this the first time you have been here?

_____

_____

d Can I get you a drink?

_____

e Please find enclosed our latest information package.

_____

_____

f We look forward to hearing from you.

_____

g You left a message yesterday – I'm returning your call.

_____

_____

Cover up each expression above and translate your sentence back into English.

Unit 6

Section A

1 Reading

Read the catalogue information about promotional calculators. Mark the sentences *T* (True) or *F* (False).

a The Pocket Size Calculator comes in two colours. ____

b The Scientific Calculator comes with batteries. ____

c The Jumbo uses a battery. ____

d The Scientific Calculator has the smallest print area. ____

e If you buy 250 Pocket Size Calculators, you pay £2.40 for each one. ____

f The Jumbo is the most expensive. ____

g You can have your company name or logo printed on the calculator. ____

h The prices don't include VAT. ____

2 Grammar

Complete the following questions by adding *is*, *do*, or *does*. The questions are about multi-colour printing and delivery costs.

a How much extra _____ it cost for a two-colour print?

b _____ there a discount for an order of more than 60?

c How much _____ the discount?

d _____ those amounts include VAT?

e _____ it the same for children's garments?

f How much _____ delivery in the UK?

g _____ that include VAT?

Calculators

CA1018   Pocket Size Calculator

Good size calculator for office and home use. Sensible sized keyboard and easy to read LCD display. To be a little different from other models, we offer this one in navy-blue colour. Look also at the price – this is good value.

50 £2.40	100 £2.25	250 £2.10

Dimensions: 125 x 68 x 20mm
Print Area: 55 x 7mm

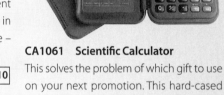

CA1061   Scientific Calculator

This solves the problem of which gift to use on your next promotion. This hard-cased calculator has 56 scientific functions explained by a detailed instruction book. It has a 10+2 LCD display, includes batteries, and has a front lid which opens up completely for easy use on a desk. An item ideal for college, school, and office use. The problem's solved!

50 £5.15	100 £4.85	250 £4.65

Dimensions: 127 x 75 x 10mm
Print Area: 50 x 50mm

CA1043   The Jumbo

Semi-desk calculator with large LCD display and large easy to use keyboard. Uses 1 'AA' battery (not included). Available in black or navy finish.

50 £5.35	100 £4.99	250 £4.90

Dimensions: 110 x 93mm
Print Area: 70 x 14mm

Pricing
The prices shown are for the quantities stated and are exclusive of VAT. If you require a larger quantity, please contact our Sales department.

Plain goods
A discount from the price is available on items bought with no print.

3 Grammar

Write questions for the following answers.

EXAMPLE
When will we get it?
You'll get it on Monday at the latest.

a _____

No, it will only take three days.

b _____

No, I'm afraid he won't be able to come.

c _____

I imagine it will take about three months.

d _____

No, I'm afraid they won't be at the meeting.
They're away in Milan tomorrow.

e _____

Yes, I can promise it will be ready by Friday.

4 Grammar

Put the verbs in brackets in the correct form to talk about the future.

a When she _____ (arrive),

I _____ (be) busy.

b Let me know when he _____
(arrive). .

c Before I _____ (leave),

I _____ (call) you.

d Call me if he _____ (arrive)
early.

e I _____ (call) you when we

_____ (finish) the meeting.

f After we _____ (receive)

payment, we _____ (send) the
goods.

g They _____ (design) the T-shirt

when they _____ (receive) the
deposit.

h How long will it _____ (take)

them to send the invoice after they

_____ (receive) the final order?

5 Grammar

Complete the questions using *have to*.

EXAMPLE
Then we have to wait a few days.
Why do we *have to wait* so long?

a I'm afraid I have to go now.

_____ so early?

b I had to leave before the end of the meeting.

_____ so early?

c I'm afraid I can't see you this afternoon. I have to
see someone.

_____ today?

d She has to be there the whole month.

_____ away so long?

6 Correspondence

Write a letter from Silvia to Marek. Cover these
points:

– Confirm the arrangements for ordering the
T-shirts.
– Explain the procedure.
– End on a positive note by saying that you are sure
the T-shirts will be a great success.

Section B

1 Reading

Match sentences **a–f** in **A** and **1–6** in **B** to make jokes.

A

a You should have been in the factory at eight o'clock. _____

b My boss is so mean that if I arrive two minutes late, he fines me. _____

c An insurance salesman has offered me a wonderful retirement policy. _____

d How many people work in your office? _____

e When does your secretary start work in the morning? _____

f The managing director offered an annual £200 prize for the best idea for saving the company money. _____

B

1 It was won by a young man who suggested that the prize should be reduced to £10 in future.
2 About two hours after she arrives.
3 Why? What happened?
4 About half of them.
5 If I make all the payments for the next twenty years, *he* can retire.
6 And if I arrive two minutes early, he charges me rent.

2 Grammar

As you read about the following methods of payment in foreign trade, put the verbs in brackets in the correct form.

Cheque

It is possible to pay an overseas supplier by cheque, but it [1]_____ (take) a long time before the supplier [2]_____ (get) his money. In a German / UK transaction, for example, the supplier could wait up to three weeks for payment.

International Giro

Payment by International Giro can be [3]_____ (make) whether the buyer [4]_____ (have) an account or not, and to a supplier whether he [5]_____ (have) an account or not. The International Giro form is [6]_____ (obtain) from any Post Office, [7]_____ (fill) out, then handed to the Post Office, who forwards the order to the Giro centre which then [8]_____ (send) the amount to a Post Office in the beneficiary's country, where the supplier [9]_____ (receive) a postal cheque.

International Money Orders

International Money Orders can be [10]_____ (buy) at most banks in the UK and are [11]_____ (pay) for in sterling or dollars. The bank [12]_____ (fill) out the order for the customer, then for a small charge, [13]_____ (hand) the IMO over, and the buyer [14]_____ (send) it to the beneficiary, i.e. the person receiving the money. IMOs can be [15]_____ (cash) or [16]_____ (credit) to the recipient's account.

Bank transfer

A home bank can also transfer money to an overseas account. If the transfer is [17]_____ (telegraph), it is [18]_____ (know) as a telegraphic transfer (T T), and if it is [19]_____ (mail), it is [20]_____ (call) a mail transfer (MT).

3 Reading

Answer these questions about the methods of payment described on page 37.

a Why is a cheque not a good method?

_____

_____

_____

b Do you need a bank account to pay by International Giro?

_____

_____

c What does the supplier receive?

_____

_____

d What does IMO stand for?

_____

_____

4 Grammar

Complete the description of SWIFT below with these prepositions:

at	for	in	on	with
by	from	of	to	

5 Vocabulary

Add these words to the table below:

buy	compete	competitor
competition	credit	creditor
debit	export	exporter
imports	insurance	insurer
insured party	salesperson	sell
supplier	supplies	
transportation	transporter	

	verb	noun	company / person
a	_____	competitiveness, _____	_____
b	_____	exports	_____
c	import	_____	importer
d	transport	transport, _____	_____
e	insure	_____	_____
f	_____	buy (a good buy)	buyer
g	supply	supply, _____	_____
h	_____	credit	_____
i	debit	_____	∅
j	_____	sale, sales	seller, _____

For the transfer ¹_____ funds ²_____ one country ³_____ another, banks ⁴_____ 151 countries participate ⁵_____ a computer-based network, known as the Society ⁶_____ Worldwide Interbank Financial Telecommunications (SWIFT). Messages are sent ⁷_____ bank ⁸_____ bank ⁹_____ high speed, but ¹⁰_____ complete security and ¹¹_____ the most economic cost, using advanced telecommunications techniques based ¹²_____ computer technology.

SWIFT has its two main operating centres ¹³_____ the Netherlands and the United States of America. These centres now link over 5,600 financial institutions (including 3,010 banks) and there are plans to expand the network even further. ¹⁴_____ average, nearly 3,000,000 payments are handled every working day. Instead ¹⁵_____ payments taking days ¹⁶_____ arrive ¹⁷_____ mail, SWIFT can deliver ¹⁸_____ minutes.

Section C

1 Telephoning

Sort the expressions below into these categories.

1 Getting through	4 Promising
a,	

2 Reasons for call	5 Leaving messages

3 Requesting	6 Polite close

a Can I speak to …, please?
b Thank you very much for your help.
c Can you send me … ?
d I'm calling about your letter of …
e Can you tell him I called?
f I'll fax that to you immediately.
g Is Mr Johnson there?
h I'm calling to ask for information about …
i I need to speak to someone about an invoice, please.
j Can you quote me a price for …, please?
k Don't worry, I won't forget.
l I look forward to seeing you then.
m Could you ask him to call me back?

2 Grammar

Write sentences using *can* or *could*.

a Ask permission to use someone's phone.

_____

b Offer to help someone.

_____

c Ask someone to call you back tomorrow.

_____

d Ask someone to fax you a copy of the agreement.

_____

_____

e Ask if it is possible for you to pay in sterling.

_____

3 Pronunciation

Tick (✓) the sentences below where *can* is pronounced in full (/kæn/).

☐ **a** My boss thinks that I *can* speak Russian, but I can't.
☐ **b** Can't you see that man over there? I *can*.
☐ **c** He can't type fast, but I *can*.
☐ **d** It's six o'clock. We *can* go now.
☐ **e** I *can* speak four languages.

4 Language check

Translate the sentences into your language.

a Shall we offer free gifts to customers?

_____

_____

b I'll be there before you arrive.

_____

c A bank in the exporter's country is selected by the importer's bank.

_____

_____

d Could I speak to Mr Wilson, please, on extension 248?

_____

_____

e I need some further information.

_____

f We are a little anxious about the delivery times.

_____

_____

g Could you confirm that, please?

_____

h Thank you. You have been most helpful.

_____

Cover up each expression above and translate your sentence back into English.

Unit 7

Section A

1 Reading

Complete the dialogue below with these phrases:

> was born   made a few   You gave us
> We got in   You were right

JAMES   Hello. How are you? Come in, come in. Did you find the house easily?

MARY   Yes, we had no trouble.
¹_____ a very good map.

JAMES   Come in and sit down. So, what do you think of Manchester?

MARY   Oh I love it. ²_____, James. You said it was a lively place.

JAMES   Well, it's my home town. I
³_____ here, you know. What time did your train get in?

MARY   ⁴_____ at three o'clock. It was on time. We checked into our hotel, ⁵_____ phone calls, and had a walk around the centre – the shops look great.

JAMES   And now you're here. What can I get you to drink? Dinner will be ready in a few minutes.

2 Grammar

Complete the sentences opposite with the past simple of one of these verbs:

buy	cost	fall	find	fly
have	leave	lend	lose	make
pay	send	take	write	

a I had a good year last year. I _____ exactly the right kind of things for my shop.

b We chose the T-shirts because they _____ less.

c Profits _____ a lot last year unfortunately.

d I _____ to New York in the morning and back again in the evening.

e I _____ time to visit the shops, too.

f I had a pleasant surprise when they _____ on time as I desperately needed the money.

g They kept their promise and _____ all the goods on the same day.

h I _____ there was a mistake in the invoice.

i I _____ the cheques to the bank and put them in the deposit account.

j We _____ early because we had to catch the last train.

k I _____ two mistakes when I filled in the form, so they sent it back.

l I _____ a lot of money when I bought too many of those silk scarves.

m He _____ me £1,000 on condition I paid him back in a month.

n They _____ to me last week and I replied immediately.

3 Grammar

Find 15 more irregular past tense verbs in the word search.

```
D  J  K  O  O  F  A  D  E  D  L  W
L  E  N  T  E  L  A  I  F  R  O  E
A  E  E  Q  U  E  R  E  B  B  S  R
I  X  W  Y  S  A  D  W  R  O  T  E
V  O  X  W  A  O  Y  O  O  U  M  P
C  U  T  H  I  P  L  N  K  G  D  T
H  G  O  H  B  I  N  D  E  H  R  E
O  A  O  F  O  R  G  O  T  T  O  X
Q  G  K  E  G  U  D  U  C  A  V  D
U  O  E  L  H  I  G  P  U  O  E  D
O  T  M  L  O  N  I  H  P  K  S  U
M  A  D  E  L  I  G  H  T  S  T  T
```

4 Vocabulary

Add *for* where necessary.

EXAMPLE

How much did you pay ̂*for* *it?*

a I expect he paid about $200 it.

_____

b I paid him $350.

_____

c I'll pay lunch.

_____

d Okay. I'll pay tomorrow.

_____

e I'll pay you back next week.

_____

f Have you paid those new gifts?

_____

Section B

1 Reading

Complete the 'subject' heading of these e-mail messages with these phrases:

> Dinner invitation   Congratulations!
> Is there anyone there?   Brainstorming meeting

a Subject: _____

We got ^{1}_____ contract! Thank you to everyone in ^{2}_____ team – you did ^{3}_____ great job.
Bob

b Subject: _____

We've had three complaints in ^{4}_____ last week about goods arriving late. I want to organize ^{5}_____ special meeting next Wednesday at 11.00 to discuss ways of improving this situation. Can you make it?
Bob

c Subject: _____

I confirm that I'll be in Hong Kong ^{6}_____ week of 15th November. Can you have dinner with me one day? How about Tuesday? Look forward to seeing you soon.
Bob

d Subject: _____

I've had no reply to my last three e-mails. Are you receiving me? Why aren't you talking to me? Have I offended you or are you having problems with your system?
Please don't leave me in ^{7}_____ dark like this!
Bob

2 Grammar

Complete the messages in **1** with the missing articles *a* and *the*.

3 Correspondence

Write the e-mail messages two people send each other on these dates and with these subject headings.

31 / 12 / 1999 16:00
Subject: New Year's Party

a _____
_____

31 / 12 / 99 16:10
Subject: Tell me more

b _____
_____

31 / 12 / 99 16:30
Subject: Are you coming or not?

c _____
_____

31 / 12 / 99/ 16:40
Subject: Depends. Bring a friend?

d _____
_____

31 / 12 / 99 16:50
Subject: Who / etc.?

e _____
_____

31 / 12 / 99 16:55
Subject: My secret

f _____
_____

31 / 12 / 99 17:00
Subject: Meeting place

g _____
_____

1 / 1 / 2000 14:55
Subject: Great party – thanks

h _____
_____

4 Reading

Look at the advertisement opposite for office software. Complete bubbles **1–5** with these verbs:

forgot	give	have	hold	is

Then match these phrases with gaps **6–10** in the text:

a need to be superhuman
b can answer him immediately
c remember them all
d contacted my colleague
e can have the details you want

Sorry — can you ¹_____ a minute?

Sorry — I ³_____ to get back to you.

Sorry — what ⁴_____ your partner's name?

Sorry — but do you ²_____ an account with us?

Sorry — I can't ⁵_____ you those figures.

Successful companies know the importance of maintaining good relationships with clients. But when they phone you, how do you ⁶_____? How do you recall their status? How do you keep in touch with them regularly? Either you ⁷_____ or you need to get Maximizer. With Maximizer you ⁸_____ on your screen in a second. Imagine a potential client has just phoned you and said, 'Hi, this is Mr Jones of XYZ Chemicals. You ⁹_____, Mr Smith, about a new contract. He's away at the moment. Can you tell me all the details?' Mr Smith!? I know twenty Mr Smiths! Maximizer is so powerful, it can find all the information you need about this Mr Smith and about XYZ Chemicals so quickly that you ¹⁰_____ as if you remembered all about them.

5 Grammar

Read the article below about Jaye Müller and put the verbs in brackets in the correct forms.

6 Reading

Mark these sentences *T* (True) or *F* (False).

a Müller didn't leave school with a clear idea of what he wanted to be. _____

b After a few years he started to sell 350,000 records every year. _____

c JFax was started when his music career was unsuccessful. _____

d He lost a lot of faxes while he was touring in England. _____

e He realized that you don't need a fax machine to have a fax number. _____

f Before JFax was created, faxes could reach you immediately if you had a PC. _____

g JFax is still a successful company. _____

Files, faxes and rock'n'roll

Nine years ago, Jaye Müller
1 _____ (leave) state school in East Germany at the age of 16, dreaming of being a rock drummer.

A few years later he
2 _____ (start) to sell 350,000 albums a year. He then
3 _____ (leave) Europe for New York. Now, at the age of 25, Müller has
4 _____ (interrupt) his music career to
5 _____ (put) a simple business idea into practice.
The idea 6 _____ (come) to him in the middle of a rock tour of English universities. The business 7_____ (be) born out of a simple frustration which is familiar to anyone working on the road. Müller
8 _____ (be) on tour for several weeks and he
9 _____ (keep) losing faxes when his band moved from town to town. One night an idea
10 _____ (come) to him. Instead of everyone owning fax machines, why didn't we just
11 _____ (have) fax numbers which automatically put documents into our PCs when we
12 _____ (log) on?
From that simple idea JFax was
13 _____ (create), and with it, the idea of the virtual office. Several rivals have
14 _____ (try) to copy JFax, but JFax is still the market leader.

Section C

1 Vocabulary

Rewrite all this information about a gsm phone as *words*.

- Up to 60 hrs standby or 180 mins talktime
- Charging time: 1 hr
- 100 name and number memories stored on a card
- Choice of 11 ring tones
- Weight: 135g
- Dimensions: L 105mm, W 49mm, D 24mm
- Price: £229.99

_____

_____

_____

_____

_____

_____

_____

2 Grammar

Do these sentences refer to the future or the present? Mark them *F* or *P*.

a I'm sorry, I'm having a meeting at the moment.

_____

b We're having dinner together tonight. _____

c Am I disturbing you? _____

d I'm seeing her later. _____

e We're having next weekend off. _____

f I'm phoning about your new gsm phones. _____

3 Telephoning

Put the words in the right order to make useful telephone expressions.

a there is Smith please Anna

_____?

b morning fax tomorrow that you to I'll

_____

c about someone need speak to I an to interview

_____

_____

d calling information to about ask prices for I'm

_____

_____

e you can me quote price a telephone the over

_____

_____?

4 Language check

Translate the sentences into your language.

a I was invited to dinner by a colleague.

_____

b I paid him £8 for it.

_____

c an average of less than five a week

_____

d Am I disturbing you?

_____

e Aren't you coming to the meeting?

_____

f I'm just ringing to say I'll be a few minutes late.

_____

_____

g That retail chain is opening a new outlet.

_____

_____

h They might need new staff.

_____

Cover up each expression above and translate your sentence back into English.

Unit 8

Section A

1 Reading

Look at this programme for a business course.

Imagine that you are attending the course. It is Sunday morning. Complete the fax below to a colleague saying what you did on Friday and yesterday and what you are doing today.

Friday evening
7.45 Dinner
9.15 Work groups: 'Getting to know you'

Saturday morning
8.45 Mission statements: Do we do what we think we do?

Sunday morning
10.00 Presentation & image: documents

Saturday afternoon
2.30 Time management
4.00 People in the front line: telephoning

Sunday afternoon
2.30 Company image

Hotel and Conference Centre

FAX

DATE:

TO:

FROM:

Hi. Arrived here on Friday evening and had a great start to the course: dinner followed by a session

1 _____

_____. We had a really good day yesterday. In the morning we had to say if we 2 _____

_____

and in the afternoon we studied 3 _____

_____ .

Both sessions 4 _____ really interesting.

This morning we 5 _____

presentation and 6 _____ .

Apart from the course, we're having a lot of fun.

See you next Friday.

---

2 Grammar

Put the verbs in brackets in the correct form to complete Teresa's letter to a friend about the course she did.

Dear Lucy,

We 1 _____ (have) a really interesting weekend last weekend. We 2 _____ (go) on a course in business practice – you know, to improve the way we 3 _____ (work). It 4 _____ (be) very interesting and we all 5 _____ (learn) a lot.

It 6 _____ (be) also nice to spend the weekend with Silvia and Marek. Marek 7 _____ (be) very nice – I 8 _____ (like) him a lot and I 9 _____ (be) quite sure Peter 10 _____ (fancy) Silvia.

The only bad thing 11 _____ (be) Peter's stupid friend Jack. I 12 _____ (not know) what Peter 13 _____ (see) in him. If you 14 _____ (ask) me, he 15 _____ (be) a real poser.

Hope to see you soon.
Best regards,

Teresa

---

3 Vocabulary

Rewrite these times in words in two ways.

EXAMPLE
11.20
eleven twenty / twenty past eleven

a 9.30

_____

_____

b 12.45

_____

_____

c 8.15

_____

_____

d 7.10

_____

_____

e 6.50

_____

_____

4 Grammar

Complete the sentences below with these words:

How much	How many	How long	What

a _____ was the last thing you did last night before you left the office?

b _____ did it take you?

c _____ hours did you spend on the report?

d _____ time will you spend on the next one?

e _____ did you think of the meeting?

f _____ people are helping you?

5 Grammar

Is *Who* the subject or object of these questions?

EXAMPLE
Who came in this morning? *subject*

a Who do you want to promote?

_____

b Who can help me this afternoon?

_____

c Who can come in tomorrow?

_____

d Who wrote the order? _____

e Who did you speak to? _____

f Who doesn't think it's a good idea?

_____

g Who does he like? _____

6 Grammar

Use the words in brackets to ask questions about the situations below.

EXAMPLE
I met their manager yesterday.
(What / you think of him?)
What did you think of him?

a I phoned the supplier earlier.
(What / he say about his last bill?)

_____

b I had lunch with the new sales manager.
(What / she say about our future?)

_____

c She only arrived two minutes ago.
(What time / leave the hotel?)

_____

d He checked everything yesterday.
(/ everything in order?)

_____

e I sent all the invitations last week.
(How many / send?)

_____

Section B

1 Reading

Read about business cards below and complete the sentences **a-f** with some of these words and phrases:

> attractive   a contract   very carefully
>
> The Partners   without thinking
>
> information only   e-mail address
>
> fax number   presenting the company image
>
> Designer Cards   a prize   aggressive

a James Beveridge works for _____ .

b His company has won _____ .

c He thinks most companies design their business

cards _____ .

d In his opinion, a business card is for

_____ .

e In his opinion, the most important piece of information on a business card is the phone

number or _____ .

f His business card is special and _____ .

2 Vocabulary

Find 15 adjectives in the word search. Sort them into the categories below.

O	A	M	B	B	E	R	Y	C	O	O	L
D	L	O	W	J	G	R	E	Y	A	I	G
W	I	D	E	C	B	E	T	E	H	O	W
N	A	E	F	L	I	R	B	L	A	C	K
G	O	R	Y	A	G	R	A	L	O	N	G
W	O	N	T	S	S	O	U	O	U	S	H
G	L	L	Q	S	U	H	I	W	L	A	D
O	W	O	D	Y	E	P	I	N	K	L	E
T	H	I	C	K	E	L	N	O	T	T	Y
M	E	I	H	E	L	E	G	A	N	T	F
T	A	L	L	I	E	R	C	A	T	E	S
P	R	O	O	K	X	Y	P	L	A	O	D

colour	size	style
yellow		

'I'm surprised how few companies think carefully about the design of their business cards,' says James Beveridge, a creative designer at The Partners, an award-winning design company. 'They think it is only a piece of card with a telephone number and address on it, and not as an image of their company. But in my opinion, the look, the feel, and the layout of a business card can all tell you a lot about how a company operates.

'When you give someone your card, you are in fact saying: "I'm available to talk to you on the phone, but if you prefer you can also contact me in other ways".'

He also points out that today a postal address is often less important than an electronic address. 'In my experience, most people use business cards to phone or send an e-mail, not to send a letter.

'Sometimes,' he says, 'people try too hard. It's incredible how little you need to do to make your card special. People immediately notice a card if you use unusual dimensions, or if you have more white space than usual.' His own card is very simple, but it is narrower than usual. It looks modern, efficient, and elegant. This is also the image the card gives of his company.

THE PARTNERS
~

Albion Courtyard
Greenhill Rents
Smithfield
London EC1M 6BN

Telephone
+44 (0)171 608 0051

Fax
+44 (0)171 250 0473

E-mail
jb@partnersdesign.co.uk

James Beveridge

3 Correspondence

In the letter below, find what is wrong with:

a the letterhead

_____

_____

b the logo

_____

_____

c the quality of printing

_____

_____

d the layout

_____

_____

e the spelling (one mistake)

_____

_____

f the punctuation

_____

_____

4 Correspondence

Number the parts of this letter in the correct order.

a Dear Ms Sturdy,

b 9 June 2000

c I am pleased to say that my partners have decided to accept the 30% trade discount you offered for a combined order and the special transport and insurance rates.

d Ms Teresa Volpe
Chief Buyer

e Re: Confirmation of Phone Order TS2

f If there is any possibility of a delay in delivery, please contact me immediately. In fact, we would very much appreciate earlier delivery if possible.

g Perfect Partners

h Ms Rachel Sturdy
Tees Total
High Street
Wooton Bassett
Nr. Swindon
Wiltshire SN4 7AB

i Could you please send us proforma invoices as soon as possible?

j Our ref: Order TS2

k Yours sincerely,

l 39–41 High Street, Highbury, London N5, England

m Further to our phone call this morning regarding a joint order for T-shirts in assorted colours and sizes, I am writing to confirm the details wc agreed. Please find enclosed our order, No. TS2 for 1,000 garments.

n Enc. order form no. XYZ2000

o Your ref: 18 May 2000

p cc Silvia Adario, Marek Staniuk, and Jack Beale

TRANSWORLD SHIPPER S
Speed is our motto

19 pudding lane
London EC 16
tel: 0181 – 9774320
fax: 0181 – 9775270

march 15th

Dear Sirs,
thank you for your enquiry re our services. I enclose a leaflet describing our services. Since the leaflet was printe there have been some changes – we now deliver to East Africa and to Sri Lanka in addition to all the other places in the leaflet. If you are interested in our services please contact Jean Smith our head of sales and she will give you a personalised quote. hoping we will have the pleasure of working with you
yours faithfully,

RJBate
MANAGING DIRECTOR.

5 Correspondence

Rewrite the following letter with appropriate punctuation and layout.

newman computers ltd 24 east street leicester leics lc8 2ef tel 011 272678 fax 011 272679 your ref 10 march 2001 our ref ah/2 appleby hotel 15 north brink road millsborough leics lg9 4pj dear sIr i am writing to confirm the booking i made over the telephone this morning i confirm that i would like one conference room with seating for 40–50 people from 830 am to 530 pm on wednesday 16th february i understand that the charge for this will be £120 if possible i would like to have the princess diana room but i would be happy with the blue room as a second choice i would like a video in the room and I understand there is an extra charge for equipment on the phone you suggested serving refreshments during the meeting could you please send me an estimate for the following coffee and biscuits at 1030 soup and sandwiches at 1245 and tea and cakes at 315 i should like to organize a dinner event in the evening could you please suggest somewhere suitable please send me written confirmation of this booking i enclose a cheque for £50 which is a non returnable deposit yours faithfully

Section C

1 Reading

Complete the 20-second course in Customer Care below with these imperatives:

say	talk	smile	make
invite	~~approach~~	offer	smile
thank	think	acknowledge	

Never treat customers as enemies.

a *Approach* them as potential friends.

b _____ of customers as guests.

c _____ them laugh.

d _____ their presence within thirty seconds.

e _____ , make eye contact, and _____ hello.

f _____ to them within the first three minutes.

g _____ product advice where appropriate.

h _____ .

i Always _____ customers and _____ them back.

2 Vocabulary

Rewrite the following sentences using the verb *get*.

EXAMPLE
Hello. Come in. Can I bring you a cup of coffee?
Hello. Come in. Can I *get* you a cup of coffee?

a I'll ask Jake to fax that to you.

_____

b I'll ask him to do it when he comes back.

_____

_____

c I'll contact you again when I hear from our supplier.

_____

_____

d What can I buy you for your birthday?

_____

3 Telephoning

Correct what B says in this telephone conversation.

A John Miller's office. Good morning.
B Hello, I am Hans Schmidt speaking. I would to speak Mr John.

1 _____

_____

A One moment, sir. I'll put you through.
B Hello, John. I call from the Germany.

2 _____

C Hello, Hans.
B You send brochure to me?

3 _____

C Yes, I sent it last week.
B No get it.

4 _____

C I'm sorry. I'll send you another one.
B I come see you.

5 _____

C Good. When?
B I come Friday in England.

6 _____

C Marvellous. I'll meet you at the airport.
B I look forward to see you Friday.

7 _____

_____

4 Language check

Translate the sentences into your language.

a What was the first thing you did on Wednesday?

_____

_____

b How long did it take?

_____

c Were you pleased with your day's work?

_____

_____

d Who really likes Peter?

_____

e Who does Marek really like?

_____

f I think they should put Special Offer first.

_____

_____

g Don't keep a caller waiting.

_____

h I'll get back to you as soon as I can.

_____

_____

i I'll get her for you.

_____

j I'll get him to call you back.

_____

Cover up each expression above and translate your sentence back into English.

Unit 9

Section A

1 Reading

Opposite is some information about sending excess baggage when you travel by air.

Find answers to these questions.

a You want to send a bicycle.

   1 What will the cubic volume of the container be?

   _____

   2 What will the dimensions be?

   _____

   3 What minimum weight will be charged for this volume?

   _____

   4 How should it be packed?

   _____

b You want to send some fragile things.

   1 What special materials are available to protect them?

   _____

   2 Where should they be packed?

   _____

c How much do extra cartons cost?

   _____

What size packing cases do I need?

1 SUITCASE =	1.5 SUITCASES = 4.5FT³	2 TEA CHESTS =
3FT³ CARTON	TEA CHEST/CARTON	9FT³ PACKING CASE

3 SUITCASES =	3 TEA CHESTS =
9FT³ PACKING CASE	13FT³ PACKING CASE

Dimensions of stock cartons and packing cases are as follows:

Description	Dimensions Imperial	Metric	Air Freight min volumetric charge
2 cu ft book carton	18/18/10 ins	46/46/25 cms	9k gs
3 cu ft carton	24/17/13 ins	59/43/33 cms	14 kgs
4.5 cu ft carton/tea chest	24/20/16 ins	61/51/41 cms	21 kgs
6 cu ft carton	24/23/18 ins	60/59/46 cms	27 kgs
9 cu ft packing case	31/22/22 ins	78/55/55 cms	39 kgs
9 cu ft bike carton	53/33/9 ins	135/84/23 cms	44 kgs
13 cu ft packing case	29/29/25 ins	74/74/64 cms	58 kgs

Picture cartons are available and can be slotted together to cover any frame up to 120cm x 120cm. Many other packing cases/crates of various sizes are available to order.

How do I pack my things?

We understand that your belongings are special so we really do everything we can to ensure that they arrive at their destination in great shape. We supply a wide variety of robust cartons and packing cases FREE OF CHARGE, in many shapes and sizes. (A nominal deposit is required which is deducted from your final bill.) We can supply bubble wrap and crepe wrap for fragile items. Please ensure that packing materials are ordered at the time of booking.

Remember: packing is a matter of common sense. DON'T overload individual items (use an extra carton – they're supplied free of charge) and DO use the recommended cases for large or fragile objects such as computers, televisions or stereos. Please use picture boxes for framed paintings and posters, and the special reinforced cartons for books. Pack delicate objects in the centre of the carton and surround with soft or protective materials. To pack bikes in their special cartons, remove the front wheel and pedals. Professional packing is available for delicate items or very large shipments. Please ask for details.

2 Vocabulary

Write these measurements and weights as words.

a 23 cms _____

b 44 kgs _____

c 120 sq cm _____

d 10 cu cm _____

e 200 m _____

f 13 km _____

g 1.12 kg _____

h 20 x 30 x 45 cm _____

_____

3 Reading

Complete the description of how Silvia's waistcoats were packed with these words:

| Then | Finally | First | Next | Before |

¹_____, despatching the waistcoats, the company packed them carefully.
²_____, they put them in individual polythene bags. ³_____, they placed ten of these bags inside a much bigger polythene bag. ⁴_____, they put this big bag inside a cardboard box and closed the box with tape. ⁵_____, they put plastic bands round the box and they sealed them with metallic clips.

4 Grammar

Underline the subject in each of the sentences in **3**, and put a ring round the objects.

EXAMPLE
... despatching (the waistcoats,) the company packed (them) carefully.

5 Grammar

Complete the description in the passive.

Before the waistcoats were despatched, they were packed carefully. They were put ...

_____

_____

_____

_____

_____

_____

_____

6 Vocabulary

Label the pictures with these words:

padding	steel drum
plastic barrel	jiffy bag
wooden crate	cardboard box

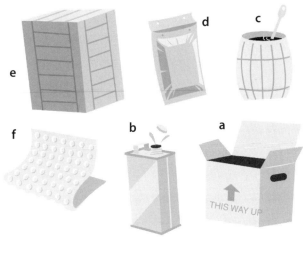

a _____

b _____

c _____

d _____

e _____

f _____

Section B

1 Grammar

Underline the correct words in brackets.

Dear Mr Harris,

I ¹(write / am writing) in connection with your recent order – see your fax 8840. Unfortunately, there has ²(been / gone) a problem with the shipment of October 7th due to the strikes at all the national airports.

This ³(means / is meaning) that we are trying to arrange alternative shipping. As you will appreciate, this may ⁴(take / to take) a little time, but we ⁵(hope / hoping) to be in touch with you again later today.

We very much ⁶(are regretting / regret) this inconvenient situation, over which we had no control. We ⁷(are apologizing / apologize) for any delay.

Yours sincerely,

Paul Wilson

Paul Wilson
Sales Manager

2 Vocabulary

Unscramble the words in brackets.

a I saw the problem (sa oosn sa) I opened the box.

_____

b There was an explosion (hte etunim) I switched on the light. _____

c It was already damaged (henw) it arrived.

_____

d I knew there was something wrong (eht tnmmoe) I took it out of the carton.

_____

3 Reading

Match these five kinds of insurance with the descriptions below.

a Credit Insurance __3__

b Insurance for Loss of Money ____

c Insurance for Loss of Profits ____

d Insurance for Goods in Transit ____

e Keyman Insurance ____

1 This insurance covers loss or damage of your goods when you transport them in your own vehicles and also when you send them by other means of delivery, such as post, road haulier, and so on.

2 If your business is heavily dependent on one or a few people for its future success, you can get this kind of insurance, for example, for a sum of £250,000 to be paid to your business in the event of one of those people dying. To get cover, you must be able to prove that the person's death would cost your firm money.

3 You don't need this type of insurance if your customers pay in cash or on delivery, but if your business depends on one or two big customers and you sell to them on credit, it will protect you if they fail to pay. However, you will probably not be able to get this insurance until you have been in business for a long time.

4 Cash and 'near-cash', such as cheques, stamps, and so on, can be insured against theft from your place of work or from the homes of directors or employees of your company, or in transit.

5 This covers you if your business is disrupted by fire or some other insured danger. It can give you money to maintain your profits, pay your employees, and pay for the extra cost of a temporary place of work.

4 Reading

Find the abbreviations (**a**–**b**) and words (**c**–**k**) below that mean:

a Bill of Lading and Bills of Lading

_____

b forwarding agents _____

c exporter _____

d importer _____

e tell someone (usually the importer) that the goods

have arrived _____

f ship _____

g the port the goods leave from

_____

h the port the goods arrive at

_____

i the symbols used to identify the goods

_____

j type _____

k the total weight _____

5 Correspondence

Fill in the Bill of Lading below with these details:

–   The name and address of the shipping company is:
    Liverpool Shipping Company
    River Street
    Liverpool
    L46 2YZ

–   The name and address of the exporter is:
    Yorkshire Woollens Limited
    Salt Mills
    Halifax
    West Yorkshire
    HX2 OEF

–   They are sending 20 boxes of pullovers weighing a total of 120 kilos and measuring 0.5 cubic metres each. Each box will be marked YW/WW Inc. New York and numbered from 1 to 20. The transport costs have already been paid at Bradford, England.

–   Write ORDER under the word *consignee* to show that the importer needs to be notified when the goods arrive in New York.

–   The name and address of the importer is:
    Worldwide Woollens Incorporated
    Fifth Avenue
    New York
    USA

–   The name of the ship is *Liver Birds* and it will sail from Liverpool to New York.

Shipper		B/L No.	666
Consignor		Reference No.	SW/ 7869
Consignee (or state 'order' to notify address)		F/A's Ref:	C/492
Notify address			
Vessel		Port of loading	
Port of discharge		Place of delivery by on-carrier	
Freight Payable at		No. of original Bs/L	
Gross weight		Measurements	
Marks and numbers		Numbers and kind of packages; description of goods	

6 Grammar

Complete the phrases below with these words:

as	by	in	to	us
as	if	the	to	with

a _____ you can imagine, we are most anxious that ...

b I would be most grateful _____ you ...

c Please let _____ know who ...

d I have returned everything _____ courier.

e I will keep everything _____ our store.

f As soon _____ I ...

g _____ minute I see her, ...

h I am faxing you _____ complain about ...

i I am writing _____ reference to ...

j We would like _____ inform you that ...

7 Correspondence

Write a polite letter of complaint about a consignment of hair dye using this information:

> Everything you ordered has arrived, but the labels for the bottles of blonde colouring have been mixed up with those for black colouring. The replacements are needed urgently. You are worried because you have already sold two bottles to customers who wanted blonde colouring. You need to know who will be responsible if your customers complain.

Section C

1 Telephoning

React to each of the sentences below by making a promise using *I'll ...* and these words:

get / call	let / know
send / immediately	see / do
fax / through in ten minutes	

a Please can you inform me as soon as it arrives?

_____

b I must have them by the day after tomorrow at the latest.

_____

c I hope you can help me.

_____

d I need that quote immediately.

_____

e I have to speak to Mr Johnson today.

_____

2 Grammar

Complete each of these sentences with *to* or *for*.

a I need _____ speak to someone about an invoice, please.

b Can you quote me a price _____ an order of 200 pieces, please?

c I look forward _____ seeing you then.

d Could you ask her _____ call me back?

e Can I speak _____ Marek, please?

f Thank you very much _____ your help.

g I'm calling _____ ask for information about your new products.

3 Reading

Read the conversation and tick (✓) the more appropriate response each time.

a Yes? Good morning. Whitworth Associates?
Good morning. Could I speak to Mr Goya, please?
- ☐ 1 What's your name?
- ☐ 2 May I ask who's calling?

b This is Anne Friar of Tecnoplate.
- ☐ 1 Hello, Ms Friar, what can I do for you?
- ☐ 2 What do you want?

c Hello, Mr Goya. I'm calling about the rooms we hired from you last week. I'm afraid we weren't really satisfied with the service.
- ☐ 1 But I thought everything was OK.
- ☐ 2 I'm sorry to hear that.

d The room was cold and the overhead projector didn't work.
- ☐ 1 But it's a new projector.
- ☐ 2 I'm sorry to hear that.

e In view of these problems, we would like a discount.
- ☐ 1 Did you ask our representative for help?
- ☐ 2 A discount! But why didn't you tell anyone about the problems at the time?

f We tried to, but unfortunately your representative wasn't in the building and we couldn't find anyone else.
- ☐ 1 I'm afraid a discount is out of the question – these were minor problems.
- ☐ 2 In that case we will of course give you a discount. Can I call you back later in the day?

4 Grammar

Complete the sentences below with *much* or *many*.

a You've got a lot of glue.

Yes, but not as _____ as I need.

b You've got a lot of paper.

Yes, but not as _____ as I need.

c You've got a lot of envelopes.

Yes, but not as _____ as I need.

d You've got a lot of ink.

Yes, but not as _____ as I need.

e You've got a lot of pencils.

Yes, but not as _____ as I need.

f You've got a lot of cards.

Yes, but not as _____ as I need.

g You've got a lot of card.

Yes, but not as _____ as I need.

5 Language check

Translate the sentences into your language.

a Which method would be best?

_____

b She wants them in three months' time.

_____

c I'd like to send them by air.

_____

d Who are they for?

_____

e Have you numbered them?

_____

f I phoned the supplier as soon as I saw the damage.

_____

_____

g Can't you do something about it?

_____

h I'll see what I can do.

_____

i I'm afraid we only have fifty available today.

_____

_____

j Oh dear, that's not as many as I ordered.

_____

_____

Cover up each expression above and translate your sentence back into English.

Unit 10

Section A

1 Grammar

Underline the correct word in brackets.

a We haven't received our payment (already / yet).
b Can't you pay me (yet / already)?
c I started learning English six months ago, and I have (already / yet) learned a lot.
d Haven't you finished it (yet / already)?

2 Grammar

Are the following *plans* or *promises*?

a We're going to buy some new equipment.

_____

b We'll give you a bigger discount.

_____

c I'll fax them now. _____

d I'm going to spend a few days visiting clients next week. _____

3 Reading

Complete the jokes below with these words:

accountant	lend	post
buying	send	will

a The world's biggest lie: the cheque is in the

_____.

b 'Can you pay me back that £10 you borrowed from me?'

'I'm afraid I can't. But I can _____ you £10 if you like.'

c 'Have you forgotten that you owe me £10?'

'No, but give me time and I _____?'

d Business is so bad these days that even people who don't intend to pay aren't _____.

e Last year it was the doctor who put me on a diet.
This year it was my ——————————.

f The taxman was surprised to receive a letter which
read, 'Dear Sir, Last year I cheated on my tax and I
can't sleep for thinking about it. I am therefore
enclosing a cheque for £2,000. If I find that I still
can't sleep, I'll —————————— you the
balance.'

Section B

1 Reading

Read the extract below about bad payers. Then
complete these notes:

1 In the early stages, it is probably best to contact
   customers in most cases by t—————— first.
   At this stage a visit can seem too h——————,
   and a letter too f——————.
2 It is important to maintain pr——————.
3 Try to talk to s——————————.
4 Ask yourself if you should u——————.
5 Think about asking for i——————————.

If customers don't pay, it is important to chase them,
because many businesses will put creditors who don't
chase them at the bottom of their list of overdue
payments. At the same time, however, it is necessary
to remain reasonable in your demands, because good
customer relations are important for future business.

There are three main ways of chasing customers for
payment – by telephone, letter, or in person. The
telephone is probably the most convenient method to
use, particularly in the early stages. It is informal,
quick, direct, and gives immediate feedback. A
personal visit will probably be as effective as a
telephone call, but in many cases it may be seen as
more hostile. Customers usually consider that a letter
is a more formal approach. It is, therefore, best used
when you feel other approaches are not effective any
more.

Other suggestions for improving debt collection
are:

1 Keep the pressure up.
2 Try speaking to someone other than your usual
  contact, such as the owner, the accountant or the
  managing director.
3 Consider using a debt collection agency.
4 Consider charging interest on any overdue debts.

2 Grammar

Put in the correct form of the verbs in brackets.

Dear Mr Beale,

I am writing further to the numerous conversations I have [1] _____ (have) with you over many months concerning our unpaid account. The amount you owe us is £8,590. On 15 November, two months after submitting the account, you [2] _____ (tell) us to forward the account to your accountant Mrs Shore for payment and we [3] _____ (send) it to her on 16 November. We [4] _____ (call) her after a week but she [5] _____ (say) she needed to discuss the matter with you and [6] _____ (promise) to get back to us.

You have [7] _____ (have) more than sufficient time to arrange for payment, so we are now thinking of putting the matter in the hands of our solicitor unless we receive immediate payment. We must insist that a cheque for the full amount is [8] _____ (send) by Monday at the latest.

Yours sincerely,

Robert Harding

Robert Harding

3 Vocabulary

Underline the time expressions that refer to the past.

a at the moment

b next summer

c since October

d by next Tuesday

e last week

f now

g after we sent the invoice

h the last time I saw her

4 Grammar

Match the two halves of the sentences.

a If you ask him,

b If you phone me about it later,

c If you decide to go with Teresa,

d If he calls,

e If you fax me the order tomorrow morning,

1 I'll give you an answer.

2 you'll be able to prepare for the meeting on the way.

3 I'm sure he'll help you.

4 I'll send everything by courier.

5 I'll tell him you're busy.

5 Grammar

Put the verbs in brackets in the correct form.

EXAMPLE
If it *arrives* (arrive) late, we will send it back.

a What will you do if he

_____ (not come)?

b I _____ (let) you know if he
gets here early.

c If there's a mistake, Jeff _____
(give) you a new invoice.

d If I pay by cash, _____ you

_____ (give) me a discount?

e They _____ (not be)
happy if they find out you've changed the colour.

6 Correspondence

Write a final demand for payment of the rental
charge on a photocopying machine.

> The machine was a ZOOM colour photocopier.
> The rent has not been paid for the last six
> months. Cost: £140 per month. If the bill is not
> paid in ten days, your company will remove the
> machine and pursue payment through a
> solicitor.

7 Grammar

Complete each sentence below with one of these
words. Only use each word once.

pay	payment	paid	pay for
paying	payment	paid	payers
payment	payable		

a Why haven't you _____ that bill
yet?

b When are you going to _____ the
T-shirts?

c Tees Total are waiting for your bill to be

_____ .

d Next time they'll ask for pre- _____ .

e In other words, they'll demand _____

up front.

f Late _____ are a nightmare in
our business.

g That invoice was _____ last
week.

h A late payment is better than a

non- _____ .

i To make some extra money, my parents are taking

a _____ guest.

j They had to _____ through the
nose for the hotel wedding reception.

Section C

1 Vocabulary

Look at the adverts below for answering machines. Find the phrases in *italics* that mean the following:

a easy to hear

_____

b in place of a cassette

_____

c tells you when the call was made

_____

d many times

_____

e recorded instructions

_____

f if you are waiting for someone to call you

_____

g you can listen to messages from a different telephone

_____

h will tell you how many calls you've had

_____

answering machines

A BT answering machine gives you the freedom to go out and get on with your life, even *if you are expecting an important call.*

All the machines are easy to use and many include microchip technology *instead of a tape* – this means every message will be *loud and clear time after time after time.*

Response 55
Digital answering machine
◆ *Voice prompts*
◆ *Time / day announcement*
◆ 14 minutes digital recording
◆ Pre-recorded outgoing message
◆ *Message counter*
◆ Remote access

£39.⁹⁹ inc. VAT

Response 5
Answering machine
◆ 30 minutes recording (15 minutes each side)
◆ Pre-recorded outgoing message
◆ Message indicator
◆ *Remote access*

£29.⁹⁹ inc. VAT

UK's No.1

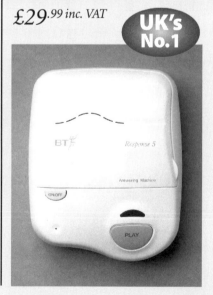

2 Telephoning

Unscramble the sentences from answerphone messages.

a calling you for thank

_____

b agents are our busy

_____

c you thank continuing hold for to

_____

d still are busy our agents

_____

e is us to your call important

_____

f you require if information services our about, two press

_____

_____

g the at afraid am I the closed switchboard is moment

_____

_____

3 Pronunciation

Do these words have long or short vowels?

EXAMPLE

it   short

a eat   _____

b these   _____

c this   _____

d car   _____

e cap   _____

f band   _____

g bar   _____

h fool   _____

i full   _____

4 Language check

Translate the sentences into your language.

a Why hasn't he paid yet?

_____

b I thought he was reliable.

_____

c They liked each other immediately.

_____

d She's already booked her ticket.

_____

e I'm going to do it tomorrow.

_____

f I'm sorry there's no one here to take your call.

_____

_____

g Please leave your name and number after the tone.

_____

_____

h We'll get back to you as soon as possible.

_____

i Thank you for calling.

_____

j If I pay in cash, will you give me a discount?

_____

_____

Cover up each expression above and translate your sentence back into English.

Unit 11

Section A

1 Vocabulary

Find the abbreviations used for the following in the job advertisements opposite.

EXAMPLE
about *c*

a accommodation _____

b agency _____

c word processor _____

d centre _____

e company (x 2) _____

f computer literate _____

g North West _____

h South East _____

i employment _____

j essential _____

k experience preferred _____

l negotiable _____

m operator _____

n part-time _____

o receptionist (x 2) _____

p required (x 2) _____

q seventeen years old or older _____

r street _____

s telephonist _____

t twenty years old or older _____

u words per minute _____

v per hour _____

w a year _____

x afternoon / evening _____

bench,
rcare
s and
es, £15

place
r, £35

£20.
£12.
15 £18

good

y suit,
, 30"

d and
C £30

RECEP/TYPIST to £12,500 17 + exp pref. 40wpm 245 8920 ABC emp agy

SECRETARY req for Estate Agents on Baker St. Accom provided 416 8888

SMALL expanding holiday comp in NW6 requires a full or pt sec. Applicants must be com lit. Salary neg. 426 7777

Stock Control Clerk c. £13,000 W1 20 + Textile Co. Will train. Call 999 0000

Tel / Rec rqd for Business Ctr. SE7. Exp pref. Sense of humour ess. £10,000pa 555 3333

WP OP £11ph. Noon-6pm SW7. Ring 741 6666 7-10pm

BASIC
condit
as new
£15. Tel
Multi-G
bar and v
pram, n.
cover. £2(
each, £60
AEG DIS
settings,
Tel: 01608
Electric s
Electric ic
Exterior ht
Tel: Didcot (
Lady's Ra
Tel:01235 3

2 Vocabulary

Put the words in the correct order to make noun phrases for advertisements.

a leading company a research

_____

b book-keeper part-time a

_____

c accounting aspects of all

_____

d letter a covering handwritten

_____

e in accessories experience selling

_____

f running office an in experience

_____

g MS Office of knowledge excellent

_____

h import-export fast-growing agency European

_____

3 Vocabulary

Look at the interviewee's answers below. Which of the categories in the table does each answer belong to?

A Skills

a

C Qualifications

b

B Experience

D Personal details

c

a I hold a current driving licence.
b I have a diploma in Office Management.
c I am single.
d I am currently working in a big London store as a shop assistant.
e I am very good with people.
f I have a high school diploma in IT.
g I can type sixty-five wpm.
h I can take shorthand.
i I am a good communicator.
j I worked in France for five years.
k I can use Microsoft Office.
l I have a certificate in computer studies.
m I live at 3, Princes Gardens, Swindon.
n I have no children.
o I can speak fluent Russian.
p I travelled around South America, teaching English for six months.
q I've done a variety of holiday jobs.

4 Grammar

Fill in the missing words.

a _____ you know Silvia?
How long have you _____ her?

b _____ you use a word processor?
How long have you _____ able to do that?

c _____ you drive?
How long have you _____ a licence?

d _____ you know him well?
How long _____ you known him?

e _____ you interested in commerce?
How long _____ you been interested?

5 Grammar

Put in *for* or *since*.

a _____ Monday   f _____ last Christmas
b _____ two years   g _____ May
c _____ yesterday   h _____ 21 May
d _____ five hours   i _____ eight months
e _____ ten minutes   j _____ 1950

6 Grammar

Put in *for* or *since*.

a I've lived in London _____ five years.
b He's worked for them _____ last July.
c I've had several part-time jobs _____ I learned to type.
d I haven't heard from her _____ before the holiday.
e How much profit have we made _____ the start of the year?
f We've known each other _____ we were at school together.
g I haven't seen him _____ a long time.

Section B

1 Correspondence

Write a letter applying for *one* of the jobs in this advertisement.

Confidential Private Secretaries (2)

The London office of this major oil company in West Africa is seeking to fill the above positions for their Executive Director and Finance Manager.

Main requirements for both positions:

Personal initiative ● Good telephone manner & effective communication skills ● Typing speed of 60/65 wpm ● Currently in employment ● Excellent knowledge of Microsoft Office ● Experienced in setting up and maintaining effective filing systems ● Between 25 and 35 years old ● Fluent Italian, French, or Portuguese is essential for the ED position, and preferable but not essential for the other vacancy.

In addition to a salary of £20–22,000 pa, the package includes pension scheme, medical insurance, 25 days holiday plus all public holidays.

Curriculum Vitae together with a handwritten covering letter should be sent to:

**W.A.O.C.
The Hailsham Building
Trendall Court
London W5**

---

2 Reading

Complete the article opposite with these verbs:

be	write	find	decide	let
make	arrange	ask	have	
have	use			

Are you a good interviewer?

Here are some suggestions about how to prepare an interview.

[1] _____ what you need to find out in the interview before you start and only [2] _____ questions that are relevant. [3] _____ prepared! Before you start, [4] _____ out as much as you can about the interviewee from the curriculum vitae and covering letter. [5] _____ down the main questions you want to ask in advance and [6] _____ them where you can see them during the interview. [7] _____ the interview go where the interviewee's answers lead to some extent, but [8] _____ your list of questions to structure the interview, and as a checklist, so that you don't forget to ask all the important questions. [9] _____ sure that you have no interruptions during the interview. [10] _____ the interview in a room where there are no distractions, such as disturbing noises. Choose and [11] _____ the chairs so that the atmosphere is neither too formal or too intimate.

3 Grammar

Complete the interview questions with these words:

are	do	have

a _____ you good at persuading people to do things?

b _____ you ever prepared displays for shop windows?

c _____ you prepared to travel abroad?

d _____ you good with your hands?

e What software _____ you have experience of?

f Why _____ you want this job?

g _____ you like being part of a team?

h _____ you ever been in an embarrassing professional situation?

i Why _____ you think you are qualified for this job?

j What languages _____ you speak?

k Why _____ you want to leave your present job?

l How much money _____ you earn in your present job?

m How long _____ you been in your present job?

n _____ you good at organizing an office?

4 Reading

Match these answers with the questions in **3**.

1 Yes, I love making things in my spare time. _____

2 French, Spanish, and Portuguese. _____

3 Yes, my friends say I am very persuasive in discussions. _____

4 Yes, I'd love to visit other countries. _____

5 Yes, lots of times. _____

6 Yes, I prefer it to working by myself. _____

7 Well, I once went to work wearing the same suit as my boss! _____

8 I think I need a change. _____

9 Well, I reorganized the office in my present job and everyone was delighted with the result.

_____

10 For nearly five years. _____

11 My basic salary is £15,000, plus bonuses. _____

12 I'd like a more challenging job than my present one. _____

13 Well, I have all the qualifications you asked for in your advertisement. _____

14 We use the latest version of Windows in my present company. _____

Section C

1 Vocabulary

How do people in Britain say these dates? Write both forms.

EXAMPLE
on 1/1/1998
*on the first of January nineteen ninety-eight /
on January the first nineteen ninety-eight*

a on 14/2/2001

_____

_____

_____

_____

b on 8/10/1851

_____

_____

_____

_____

c on 23/8/1975

_____

_____

_____

_____

d on 31/7/1933

_____

_____

_____

_____

2 Telephoning

Number the parts of this telephone conversation in the right order:

☐	**a**	Speaking.
☐	**b**	I'm phoning on behalf of Mr Staniuk. I'm afraid he'll be away on Monday, so he won't be able to see you then.
1	**c**	Good morning. Can I speak to Bob Watson, please?
☐	**d**	Oh dear, I wanted to meet him as soon as possible.
☐	**e**	Goodbye.
☐	**f**	And can you please remember to bring four copies of your report?
☐	**g**	Could you manage another day next week?
☐	**h**	Would Wednesday afternoon be convenient, at three o'clock?
☐	**i**	Yes, I'm free on Wednesday.
☐	**j**	Yes, that's fine.
☐	**k**	Yes, of course. So that's Wednesday at three o'clock with four copies of the report. Okay. Bye.

3 Telephoning

Use the dialogue in **2** to write a message from Mr Staniuk's secretary telling him about the new time for his meeting with Bob Watson.

📞 **Message**

_____

_____

_____

_____

_____

_____

_____

_____

_____

_____

_____

4 Vocabulary

Complete the sentences below with one of these prepositions of time:

after	at	by	for	in	on	since

a Our meeting is ———— Wednesday ———— eleven o'clock.

b Looking forward to seeing you ———— May.

c I'm afraid I'll arrive ———— your presentation is finished.

d I've been so busy ———— nine o'clock this morning.

e Can you send them to reach me ———— the end of April at the latest?

f We will send you our new catalogue ———— the spring.

g We had our last meeting ———— the end of the month.

h I was just ———— time for the meeting.

i We've been in business ———— more than twenty years.

j We launched it ———— 1978.

k The appointment is ———— ten o' clock ———— the tenth of August.

l They waited an hour ———— you, but then they started the meeting.

5 Language check

Translate the sentences into your language.

a Are you good at organizing an office?

_____

_____

b Have you ever prepared displays for shop windows?

_____

_____

c Why do you want to leave your present job?

_____

d Marek has worked in England for a few months.

_____

_____

e We've sold a lot of these since the beginning of January.

_____

_____

f I speak English fluently and have a good level of French.

_____

_____

g I'm afraid I won't be able to see you tomorrow.

_____

h Would Thursday be convenient?

_____

i I'm calling on behalf of a friend.

_____

j Can he manage another day?

_____

Cover up each expression above and translate your sentence back into English.

Unit 12

Section A

1 Grammar

Put the verbs in brackets in the correct forms.

a Will you let me _____ (use) the phone, please?

b He persuaded me _____ (buy) two copies instead of one.

c Can you ask him _____ (come) an hour later?

d They made me _____ (do) a test.

e I must get them _____ (send) some more by express.

f Good news! They'll let us _____ (pay) a month late.

2 Vocabulary

Complete these sentences with *make* or *do*.

a Peter hopes to _____ a lot of money.

b Can you _____ me a favour?

c They want to _____ a go of the shop.

d Can you _____ a decision before Friday?

e I want to _____ a business course.

f Don't _____ any mistakes!

g May I _____ a suggestion?

h I can _____ without it.

i May I _____ a call?

j It doesn't _____ sense.

k That'll _____ you a millionaire.

l You _____ me laugh.

m Can you _____ me a coffee, please?

3 Reading

Read about working in a record shop. Match each sentence with a gap.

a We actually get a lot of applications from people with degrees in music and media studies.

b Of course, if you apply for a job, you will be expected to have an interest in music.

c What's the difference between selling a tin of tomatoes and the latest Rock CD?

d Some customers do take things without paying.

e Marie Steadman, 21, is typical of the Virgin store's 170 employees.

Going for records

1 *c* Not much, say some music critics. But for the young people thinking of working in shops, selling records will always be Number One.

One of the world's largest music stores is the Virgin Megastore in London's Oxford Street. According to the personnel manager, you don't need qualifications coming out of your ears!

2 _____ But what's really important is maturity, an ability to get on with the public and, ideally, some experience of working in shops, but not necessarily record shops,' she says.

3 _____ One chain, Our Price, actually give you a mini

'Pop Quiz' before you get an interview! Lots of applicants play in a band or have a record collection or, if nothing else, at least follow the charts.

4 _____ Arriving in London to look for work, she quickly found herself taking thousands of pounds a day for Virgin.

5 _____ But most are honest, friendly, ready to share a joke, or even generous – Marie was given a £25 ticket for a pop concert by one customer. And sometimes they are also famous. Often the best customers are DJs from abroad, who can spend up to £400 on records in a single visit.

4 Reading

Tick (✓)the best response to the customer's complaints.

a I'm afraid I have a number of complaints about the service on the flight.
- ☐ 1 How many complaints? What is wrong exactly?
- ☐ 2 Well we are very short-staffed at the moment.
- ☐ 3 Oh. I'm sorry to hear that, Sir.

b I ordered a vegetarian meal but I didn't get it.
- ☐ 1 Perhaps you ordered it too late. You have to order it a week in advance.
- ☐ 2 That is very annoying. I'll look into it and find out what happened.
- ☐ 3 But there was only a little meat in the meal.

c The seats were very small.
- ☐ 1 That's interesting, Sir. Thank you for giving us your opinion.
- ☐ 2 Well, you are rather bigger than our average passenger, Sir.
- ☐ 3 What do you expect if you travel economy?

d There were a lot of babies crying.
- ☐ 1 Well no one else complained.
- ☐ 2 Yes, I'm sorry about that. There aren't normally so many on a flight.
- ☐ 3 Well, you were a baby once.

e You hadn't got the perfume I wanted in the in-flight boutique.
- ☐ 1 We can't stock everything!
- ☐ 2 It's a very old-fashioned perfume.
- ☐ 3 I'm afraid there is not much demand for that kind of perfume, but it is *my* favourite.

Section B

1 Grammar

Complete these sentences with *who* or *which*.

a Jeff, _____ lives next door, is an accountant.

b My sister, _____ lives in Paris, is a teacher of commercial English.

c This new machine, _____ we bought in Poland, works very well.

d Marek, _____ has travelled a lot, has never been to Canada.

e The next bus, _____ goes to the station, stops round the corner

2 Correspondence

Read the letter below and underline the most appropriate expressions in brackets.

Dear Sir,

I [1](am pleased / regret) to inform you that once again you have sent us the wrong goods. This is the third time this year that we have had to [2](complain / congratulate you). Your mistake has caused us great inconvenience and has brought us [3](new customers / the loss of some customers). In view of this, we have no alternative but to cancel [4](our first order / the remaining orders) and look for a new and more reliable [5](customer / supplier).

We are sending back the [6](consignment / presents) we received yesterday together with your invoice. We are sorry to do this but you leave us no alternative.

Yours faithfully,

Jack Gottard

Jack Gottard

3 Correspondence

Read the reply to Jack's letter and underline the most appropriate expressions in brackets.

Dear Mr Gottard,

Thank you for your 1(letter / order) of 5 May 1999. We are very sorry for the inconvenience we have 2(had / caused you) and we apologize. The mistakes were due to 3(a new computing system in our warehouse / new management) which has caused a lot of problems. We have now solved these problems and are confident that 4(nothing like this / things like this) will go wrong in future.

We ask you to 5(confirm / reconsider) your decision to cancel your orders. We would like to offer you a 20% discount on all orders for the next eighteen months to show that we 6(value your custom / really need you).

We look forward to hearing from you soon.

Yours sincerely,

James Sapley

James Sapley

4 Correspondence

Write a reply to a letter of complaint using this information.

- On March 2nd in consignment no. 662 you sent the wrong amount of English dictionaries.

- You sent double the quantity of the version for young children and only half the adult version.

- Unfortunately, the adult version is now out of stock and you don't expect more copies to be available before August.

Section C

1 Telephoning

Write out this telephone conversation in full.

EXAMPLE
You work at the Rex Hotel. Answer the phone.
Good morning. Hotel Rex. Can I help you?

a States reason for phoning – to book a room 9/8–16/8.

CALLER _____

_____

b Ask what kind of room they want – single or double.

YOU _____

_____

c Says what kind of room is required.

CALLER _____

_____

d Give the price (£85 per night, breakfast included).

YOU _____

_____

e Accepts the price and asks if a deposit is required.

CALLER _____

_____

f Explain that the deposit is the price of one night in the hotel.

YOU _____

_____

g Promises to send a cheque immediately.

CALLER _____

_____

h Thank your customer. Express your pleasure that he will be staying with you. Finish the call.

YOU _____

_____

_____

2 Grammar

Complete the questions using *(be) going to*.

EXAMPLE
Someone has offered your friend a new job.
You ask: (take it)?
Are you going to take it?

a Your boss has to buy a number of computers.
You ask: (How many / buy)?

_____

b Your friend is going to an interview for a new job.
You ask: (What / wear)?

_____

c Your friend's boss is thinking of sending him to an important conference.
You ask: (send you by yourself)?

_____

d You don't understand why your colleague is planning to leave.
You ask: (Why / leave)?

_____

e Your colleague's husband has decided to buy a new car.
You ask: (What car / buy)?

_____

3 Grammar

Complete the sentences with *(be) going to*.

a I / do a course on office technology.

_____

_____

b He / travel around Australia after that.

_____

c I / not go to university. I never want to study again!

_____

_____

d I / look for a job.

_____

e They / celebrate winning that new contract.

_____

_____

f He was so rude to me yesterday! I / not speak to him again.

_____

_____

4 Telephoning

How much do you remember about when Peter calls Manuel? Complete the dialogue by putting the words in brackets in the correct order.

PETER   Hello, Manuel, it's Peter from England.

MANUEL Hello, Peter, (call I'll Silvia)

¹ _____ .

PETER   No, no. (you to to I speak want)

² _____ .

Listen. (on I'm coming Sunday)

³ _____ .

MANUEL Sunday.

PETER   That's right, on Sunday afternoon. (But Silvia tell mustn't you) ⁴ _____ .

_____ . I want it to be a surprise.

MANUEL A surprise. Why?

PETER   I want you to do something for me. (secret you a keep can) ⁵ _____

_____ ?

MANUEL Of course. But ... (do what you to going are)

⁶ _____ ?

PETER   (to am I take going Silvia out)

⁷ _____ .

Can you book me a table at a good restaurant?

MANUEL (El Limonero you do know the)

⁸ _____ ?

PETER   Yes, that would be perfect. For nine o'clock. Table for two, Manuel.

5 Reading

Below is a sales talk that Teresa and Marek give at a trade fair. Match each phrase opposite with a gap.

a listen to us today
b and gentlemen
c she bought for
d a small Italian town
e What we need
f of the same old products
g on their own
h terribly expensive
i a strong tradition
j they are made of
k than an antique
l a certain amount of our products
m an original painting
n for example

Ladies ¹___. Thank you all for giving your time to come and ²___ .We have a simple message. We feel that the gift shop market is tired ³___ on sale all over the world. If you walk into a gift shop in Amsterdam, it's the same as a shop in London or even in ⁴___ .

You carefully choose a present for your friend, and what happens when she opens it? She finds exactly the same thing as ⁵___ her mother. You bought it in London; she bought it in Siena, but it's exactly the same thing, and that's bad news. ⁶___ is small suppliers who will give us original things. But where are these suppliers? It takes a lot of work to find small craftsmen working ⁷___ in different countries. That's where we come in. We will do the hard work for you. We have extensive contacts in Italy, in Poland, and in Spain. Three countries with ⁸___ of craftsmanship. We will supply a small number of shops and exclusivity agreements will be available on a geographical basis.

Doesn't that mean they'll be ⁹___ ? Is that what you're asking yourselves? No. If we have a commitment from our outlets to buy ¹⁰___ every year for a period of, say, three years, I am sure we can keep prices down. All we need from you would be a letter of intent.

Now I'm going to show you some of the kind of things we're talking about. Take these clocks, ¹¹___ . Each one is unique. They are hand-painted by craftsmen in a village in Italy. They are individually signed. Look at the wood ¹²___ – each piece of wood comes from a known source. This piece of oak was a window in a small house in the village. It's at least two hundred years old. It's cheaper ¹³___ but as individual as ¹⁴___ .

6 Reading

To convince a bank to lend him money, Marek has to prepare a *business plan* with these sections:

a Marketing policy
b The Product or Service
c Operational details
d Financial analysis
e His past experience
f Management policy
g Future prospects

The extracts below are from his business plan. Match each extract with a section from the plan.

1 ____
The service consists of providing a link between owners of gift shops who are looking for original items and craftsmen who are looking for markets.

2 ____
With pleasant premises in Covent Garden, paid for for the next two years by Mr Staniuk's backers and attractively furnished, the company will operate from London.

3 *a*
Publicity will be a mixture of word of mouth (the director has a network of connections in the retail business) and presence at trade fairs. Some direct mailing will be considered especially at the beginning of the activity.

4 ____
To interest big retail chains in the products would be to defeat the object. However, forecasts show that the investor can expect a modest but constant return on his investment.

5 ____
Risks are low – Mr Staniuk has already rented premises and can cover the rent for the next two years; the main costs will be running costs. He will not have to tie money up in stock as he will essentially be providing a service.

6 ____
Marek Staniuk has experience of selling in the retail section in Gdańsk. He has already introduced a wide range of locally produced goods into the international market through his connection with the Perfect Partners Group, of which he is a founder member.

7 ____
The Managing Director will report to a board consisting mainly of his backers but including two expert advisers as well as a representative from the Polish authorities.

7 Language check

Translate the sentences into your language.

a I'm afraid it is not our policy to give a refund.

_____

_____

b Would you like to exchange it for another colour?

_____

_____

c Could you ask them to come back later?

_____

_____

d Can you let me know as soon as possible?

_____

_____

e What can I do to help?

_____

f This doesn't make sense.

_____

g That is our new Sales Manager, who comes from Spain.

_____

_____

h This is our latest catalogue, which describes all our products.

_____

_____

i How would you like to pay?

_____

j I'm sorry, I didn't catch your surname.

_____

Cover up each expression above and translate your sentence back into English.

Unit 13

Section A

1 Grammar

Below is a list of questions to ask yourself if you are considering a franchise. Complete the questions with these words:

is / are	does / do	has / have

a How long _____ the franchisor been in franchising?

b What _____ the backgrounds of the directors?

c _____ the franchisor have the financial resources to sustain the network?

d Who _____ the franchisor's bankers?

e How many existing franchisees _____ there?

f _____ the franchisor happy to provide you with a list of the names and addresses of all existing franchisees so that you can talk to them?

g How many franchisees _____ failed? Why?

h Who _____ the main competitors?

i How _____ they compare in terms of price, quality, delivery, and service?

j _____ there a market in your area for your chosen franchise's goods or services?

k _____ there been any market research?

l _____ the franchise operating in a market subject to fashion, or is there a long term market for your goods or services?

m _____ the business seasonal?

n _____ there fixed opening times?

o If so, what _____ they?

p What territory _____ being offered? Is it postcode-based or geographically-based?

2 Grammar

Put the verbs in brackets in the correct form to talk about hypothetical situations.

a If I _____ (have) some money, I _____ (buy) a motorbike.

b What _____ you _____ (do) if you _____ (have) more free time?

c If you _____ (inherit) a shop, what _____ you _____ (sell) in it?

d If you _____ (can) do any job you wanted, what job _____ you _____ (choose)?

3 Reading

Complete the questions below with these words:

attract	be	choose	employ
need	organize	play	prefer
put	sell	specialize	want

4 Reading

Answer the questionnaire with your own ideas.

If you had a clothes shop in your town, how would you run it?

1 Would you _sell_ clothes to men or women, or both? _____

2 What age-range would you _____, for example: 0–5, teenagers, 20–30, over 50? _____

3 Would you _____ in tall people, or people who are over-weight? _____

4 What price-range would you _____, for example: very cheap, cheap, middle-range, expensive, very expensive? _____

5 In what part of your town would you _____ to have your shop? _____

6 If the shop had two rooms of, say, eighty square metres each, how would you _____ the furniture (shelves, cupboards, hangers, tables, cash desk, umbrella stand, plants, etc.)? _____

7 What would you _____ in the windows? _____

8 What music would you _____ in your shop? _____

9 If your shop was not in the main street, how would you _____ people to come into it? _____

10 Who would you _____ to work in the shop? _____

11 Would their appearance _____ important? _____

12 What qualifications would they _____ to have? _____

Section B

1 Vocabulary

Complete the sentences below with these words. Use each word once only.

alternatively	and	as	even if
furthermore	however	which	

a This is to acknowledge receipt of the two parcels, _____ arrived this morning.

b I'm afraid I can't come to the meeting later _____ I have a visitor from Poland.

c _____, if you need to talk to me urgently, you can call me on my mobile.

d I don't want to risk it, _____ there is the chance of making a big profit.

e You could come by train directly to central London. _____, I could pick you up at Stansted Airport.

f I like Peter _____ I like Teresa. I like them both.

g We can help you with market research. _____, our staff are available at all times to give advice on other matters.

2 Vocabulary

Solve the anagrams in the following letter.

Dear Mr Polanski,

Thank you for your letter, which arrived this morning. I have read the proposed
1 _____ (ttaoccnr) and am pleased to say I accept all its
2 _____ (emrts).

However, I do have a problem with the
3 _____ (eedlivyr) dates. I am afraid that we will not be able to deliver the first 4 _____
(nnnigscmeot) before the twentieth. This is because of a problem we are having with our 5 _____ (spiuelrps) and I am sure that in future we will be able to deliver as 6 _____ (dtiuslaept) on the fifth of the month.

I enclose a signed 7 _____ (ypoc) of the contract and hope that the variation in the first delivery date will not cause you too much 8 _____ (cnecvnnioeien).

Yours 9 _____ (eeiylrcns),

Martin Bell

Martin Bell

3 Correspondence

Write a reply to the letter in **2**. Make these points:

– You have received the signed contract and you appreciate the problem Martin Bell is having with his suppliers.

– You are not worried about this, as long as he can guarantee delivery on the twentieth of this month and on the fifth of every subsequent month.

Section C

1 Reading

Read the article below and correct these statements.

EXAMPLE
In the game the players build a tower.
No, the players start with a tower.

a Last year 3 million people played Jenga.

_____

b The tower is made of plastic bricks.

_____

c All the bricks are the same size.

_____

d Leslie Scott lived in England when she was young.

_____

e Friends in Ghana got extra sets made for her.

_____

f Her first job in England was in advertising.

_____

g Her first London exhibition was a big success.

_____

h In 1993 Jenga sold well in England, and later in America and Canada.

_____

SUCCESS was a long time coming for Leslie Scott, the creator of Jenga, the second best-selling game in the world. It was only thanks to financial support from her mother, an understanding bank, and good friends that she was able to persevere.

The object of Jenga, a game of 54 wooden bricks, is to take blocks from the bottom of a tower and put them on the top without making it fall over. Last year 3m people bought it – only Monopoly was more popular.

As a child, Scott lived in Africa, where she spoke Swahili as well as English. Jenga is a Swahili word meaning 'to build'. She invented the game at the age of 20 for her eight-year-old brother, Malcolm, while she was living in Ghana. 'We had these handmade wooden bricks that were all slightly different in size. This is critical as Jenga doesn't work if they're all the same size. It's a fun game but quite intricate. We got a number of sets made for friends and played with them after dinner at home.'

Back in England, she worked in marketing, but at 25 she gave up her job to launch Jenga, not realising how hard it would be. Lloyds Bank lent her £30,000, and her mother lent her £12,000. When she first exhibited the game at a toy fair in London, there was little interest, but she didn't lose hope. She borrowed more and more money, including two more bank loans. When she was 30, the game started selling in Canada, thanks to a friend's brother, but only slowly. Then two years later an American toy giant started selling the game under licence, and at first that

brought in a few thousand dollars a year. In 1993, however, the game made serious money in America and Canada and soon afterwards the American company launched the game on to the British market and sales took off. Since then royalties worldwide have rolled in.

2 Vocabulary

What do the words in **A** mean in the article on page 79? Match them with their definitions in **B**. Look back at the article to help you.

A		**B**	
a	support	**1**	continue trying
b	persevere	**2**	help
c	more popular	**3**	a little
d	as well as	**4**	complicated
e	slightly	**5**	permit
f	intricate	**6**	in addition to
g	gave up	**7**	liked by more people
h	launch	**8**	a lot of money
i	lent	**9**	payments for sales of an invention
j	bank loan	**10**	start to sell a new product
k	borrowed	**11**	an amount of money lent by a bank
l	license	**12**	took money that had to be given back later
m	serious money	**13**	gave money which had to be paid back later
n	royalties	**14**	left

3 Vocabulary

Write these number expressions from the Jenga article in words.

a 54 _____

b 3m _____

c 20 _____

d 25 _____

e £30,000 _____

f £12,000 _____

g 30 _____

h 1993 _____

4 Language check

Translate the sentences into your language.

a If I won a lottery, I would buy into a fast food franchise.

_____

_____

b There are two ways of doing this.

_____

c I could sell at least 120 units a year.

_____

d I would be able to offer you a price of £58 per unit.

_____

_____

e To win, you must land on square 40.

_____

f If you don't answer correctly, you don't move.

_____

_____

g You can have another go.

_____

h How do you spell that?

_____

i What's the missing word?

_____

j What's the name of the document I need to fill in?

_____

_____